CHRISTIAN FOLK LITERATURE

The Plowboy
Words of Faith and Encouragement

Patrick Martin Williams, Jr.
Edited by Vana J. Plaisance

XULON PRESS

"Stay away from a wisdom that will not let you laugh, a philosophy that will not let you cry, and a greatness that will not let you bow before little children."
- Patrick Martin Williams Jr.

This book is dedicated to the author's late mother, Sarah Johnson Lewis Williams, of Kentucky, U.S.A., and to all other Christian mothers, living or deceased, around the world. May all mothers and fathers be prayerful.

Contents

Introduction

By Vana J. Plaisance

Vana and P. M. Williams, 1968

In my memory Patrick Martin Williams Jr., 1898-1988, my maternal grandfather, was a hard worker, a good citizen, a devout Christian, a theologian, a philosopher, a historian, an interesting storyteller, a humorist, a wise counselor, a compassionate caregiver and the greatest of friends.

A native of Lee County, Kentucky, he was born in a log cabin on Shuemaker Ridge, in the area known as Zoe. His family claimed to be descendants of the schoolmaster named Williams who taught President George Washington, as noted in Encyclopedia Britannica (1965). This claim was reportedly confirmed by Hubert Curtis Williams while conducting research to establish the family's genealogy.

During adolescence, Patrick Martin Williams Jr. left his humble home in the Appalachian hills of Kentucky with just thirty-four cents and the clothes on his back, moving to Beattyville. He acquired a job in a livery stable and completed high school. The young Patrick continued his studies at Fugazy Business College, Lexington, and eventually made his home in the central bluegrass city of Winchester. After working for railroads for about fifty years, he retired from the C & O Railroad Company. He was a member of First Christian Church and the Masonic lodge.

Grandfather was acquainted with many hardships and sorrows. He outlived three wives: Fannie Roberts Williams, Lula Wright Williams and Cea Billiter Williams. With Fannie he had two children: Norman B. Williams and Patrick Rudolph Williams. With Lula he also had two children, Sarah Catherine Williams and Hubert Curtis Williams. He had six grandchildren: Patrick Joseph Williams, a church pastor in Winchester, and Kim Williams, sons of Rudolph; April Katherine Bishop and Vana Carol Johnson, daughters of Sarah; and David Curtis Williams and Debra Williams, the children of Hubert.

Following Sarah's debilitating car accident, Grandfather reared my sister, Kathy, and I while caring also for our grandmother, Lula. Later, while in his sixties, Grandfather was a victim of a car accident, too, resulting in three fractures to his neck and back. He said it was one of several times throughout his life in which he narrowly escaped death. Eventually, after the accident, Grandfather was able to walk again and to care for Grandmother, who was confined for many years to a wheelchair due to rheumatoid arthritis. She was a retired school teacher, having graduated from college at Bowling Green. I never saw Grandmother walk. On her headstone, Grandfather wrote, "She held no bitterness in life's suffering, only self-giving love."

On his own headstone, my sister and I requested a familiar and poignant quote from Grandfather: "Stay away from a wisdom that will not let you laugh, a philosophy that will not let you cry, and a greatness that will not let you bow before little children." It says so much about him.

When I was an adolescent, Grandfather wrote a manu-script for a Christian book, which he titled *The Plowboy*. After attempting to have his book published in the 1960s, a time of great social unrest, Grandfather entrusted his beloved original manuscript to my care—with my promise that I would strive to have his work published someday. Many of Grandfather's familiar stories were not contained in his manuscript. For example, his two grandfathers fought against each other in the Civil War. Notably during Grandfather's lifetime America was involved in several wars, including World War I, World War II, the Korean Conflict and the Vietnam War. Consequently, one of his predominant themes in *The Plowboy* is peace and safety for all.

Regrettably it took me forty years to fulfill my promise to have his work published. Since Grandfather passed away in 1988 at the age of 89, he did not live to see his book published. But his spirit lives on in my memory and on the pages of his beloved book, *The Plowboy*. May my Grandfather's insights into Bible verses, his reflections on life, his stories, his prayers and his jokes be as much of a blessing to you as they have certainly been to me, to his other family members, and to the many people fortunate enough to have known Patrick "Pat" Martin Williams Jr.

Prologue

Hello, boys and girls, men and women. Hello, world. It is good to be here. It is good to be alive on this day, a day the Lord has made. Let us be glad and rejoice in it with happiness, joy, righteousness, peace, love and service in the Holy Spirit. This is the kingdom of God, which you could not have without God and man.

I am Chum Sibun—Chum, meaning a friend, and Sibun, meaning seven—meaning I am a friend to God and a friend to man. Now I am also the little bare-footed boy of seven years of age that wanted to plow for his father at the beginning of this twentieth century.

I have started this book on my late mother's one hundredth birthday.

* PART ONE *

THE GREAT GOAL

Supremacy of the Bible and a Christ-centered Program

*We can seek, find and hold—from now to the end of time—
but to no avail unless we have the supremacy of the Bible
in our works, deeds and lives, as well as a Christ-centered
program in our lives, not in our words alone.*

Wedding Day:
Lula Catherine Wright and Patrick Martin Williams Jr.

CHAPTER 1

Grace and Forgiveness
❖❖

*My grace is sufficient for thee: for my strength is made
perfect in weakness.*
2 Corinthians 12:9

After asking my father to let me plow—for it seemed
so easy to him and also to me—he would say, "You
are too little to plow. You will have to drink a lot of cups of
sweet milk and eat a lot of cornbread before you can plow
for Daddy. When you get big enough to plow I will let you
plow."

"Yes, Father, but I want to plow today," I pleaded. "I can
thin corn."

"Yes, Chum, you are a good corn thinner, and the day
will come when you will make a good plowboy. But you will
have to wait and help us eat a lot more hog and hominy."

So I went on to my corn thinning with plowing on my
mind and wishing I could show Father just how good I could
plow for him.

I had not reached the upper end, the other end, of the
corn row in the cornfield when I looked up and saw Uncle
Bill Olanger coming with his plow and coulter for Father to
sharpen in the blacksmith shop. That was a part of Father's

job, to do all kinds of blacksmith work for everybody: sharpening their plows, shoeing their horses, building and repairing their wagons and all the other things—too numerous to mention—that went with the blacksmith trade.

When I got back to the lower end, the horse and plow were turned at the end ready to go in another corn row to plow. Father and Uncle Bill were at the shop by that time, and I could hear the bellows blow and the sound of the hammer on the anvil as Father sharpened the plows.

Now then, I said to myself, I can plow with the plow stock my father made. It was a single plow stock, and Father had one of the best plow horses anywhere. So I reached up to the plow handles; my head was not above the plow handles.

I clucked to old Tim, but he would not move. I said, "Go on!"

The horse just looked back, as if to say with that horse sense, "Are you a plowboy?"

By that time I was getting impatient, so with a louder voice—and perhaps, I thought, a more manly voice—I yelled, "Get up!" Good old Tim thought perhaps I meant it—I was in earnest—so he started. But I could not hold the plow straight.

It went to the right and plowed up some corn. I tried to straighten it up, but it went to the left, plowed up some corn, and so on before I could get the horse stopped. I was awfully busy or awfully scared, one or both, but I finally thought of the word to stop the horse. Almost out of breath and almost out of strength as well I yelled, "Whoa, Tim!" and Tim stopped.

All right now. Old Tim looked back at me again, as if to say with his horse sense, as if to say, "Now you see" or "Now you've done it." Honestly, if my plowing stock or my plowing ambition could have been placed on the New York Stock Exchange, I don't believe it would have sold for two cents a share.

Talk about being willing to thin corn. I have never, to my recollection in life, loved to thin corn as fast and as willingly as I did then. By the time I made my round, Father was back from the blacksmith shop. We both got there to the same spot at the same time. Chum, the boy who wanted to plow, did not want justice. He wanted mercy.

My eyes were filled with tears, and tears were running down my cheeks, streaked and soiled of the good earth from those little dirty, corn-thinning hands. Yet, knowing Father as I did, I thought I knew what I would get. Father looked at my plowing. Honestly it looked like a cyclone had struck those two rows of corn: one row to my right and one row to my left.

"Father, forgive me. I am so sorry. I wish I had not tried to plow," I said with tear-dimmed eyes and in broken sobs of grief. "Father, please do not whip me too hard. I only have on my new shirt Mother made on her fingers for me. If you hit me too hard, it will cut the blood out of my back through this thin cotton shirt."

By that time Father was crying himself. "God bless my boy," he said. "I did not know he could plow so well."

Once I was young, and now I am old, but that was a day I have never forgotten. I have never known such joy and happiness, sorrow, regret and grief before or after that day in the first part of the twentieth century.

Father went on to his plowing, wiping the tears from his eyes with a red bandana handkerchief from his right hip pocket, and I went on to thinning corn with all my tears dried.

CHAPTER 2

Serving God: Better to Wear Out Than Rust Out

I have always wanted to serve God—and I have done about the same job serving God as I did plowing for my father—but I am hoping, trusting and praying my name will be written in the Lamb's Book of Life. When God is through with us here on earth, He will hand us down to our graves in great peace; and on that resurrection morning we will be among the first in Christ to rise. Then, if we could faithfully serve Him, God might say, "I did not know you could serve Me so well. Enter into that upper and better kingdom prepared for you from the foundation of the world to all that love and keep my commandments."

It is hard to give that which you do not have. I have a desire to give some of the best that is in me, to all people everywhere, especially our boys and girls. They are the finest investment in the world. May God bless them with health, intelligence, character and a willingness to work; for work will win and faith will work wonders.

To obey the commands of Christ is a great and daring faith.

Jesus said, **"If ye love me, keep my commandments"** (John 14:15).

Jesus said, **"Ye are my friends, if ye do whatsoever I command you"** (John 15:14).

Character is like white paper: Once soiled, it is hard to clean. It is easier to keep it clean than it is to soil it and then try to clean it. It smears so badly.

My hope and trust is that the youth, the adults and the elderly might be with God and not separated from God. For man to separate himself from God is bad, but for God to separate Himself from man is worse.

Consider these words: from, through and into. Trained, dressed and presented.

Where are we from? Why are we here? Where are we going?

When is the proper time to begin to train a child? To me, a thousand years before it was born would not be any too soon, if you want to take into consideration both the physical and spiritual, as well as all the other important factors too numerous to mention.

Work, play, worship and love are also among the things that belong to God. With them we will live, but without them we will die. If just one were taken away from us, where would we be? Also, health, character, intelligence and a willingness to work: Now then, if just one of those things mentioned were taken away from us, where would we be?

We do not pay money for all the good, meaningful and necessary things of life. If you think so, let us name a few and think upon them: sunshine, rain, freshness of the air. If only one were taken from us, where would we be?

Our wonderful girls and boys: We are so proud of them and thankful for them. Let us, by the help of God, leave nothing undone to help them get an education, for that little piece of paper the degree is on will open doors for them.

Jesus said, **"Ask, and it shall be given you; seek, and ye shall find; knock, and it shall be opened unto you"** (Matthew 7:7).

Work will win, and faith will work wonders. To obey the commands of God is a great and daring faith. Boys and girls, do not misunderstand me and think education is all and the most important goal. Not by any means. With it—but without Christ—you are nothing. With it—and with Christ—that is sufficient. Christ is our sufficiency, for an individual or for the world.

It is an individual affair to receive Christ as the Son of God, and as your master, teacher, redeemer, Lord and Savior, the one who loved us so and believed in us so much that He gave His life for our redemption. He was the friend and the master of men. Behold the Lamb of God, who takes away the sin of the world, who saves the lost and who strengthens the saved.

Jesus said, **"For I am not come to call the righteous, but sinners to repentance"** (Matthew 9:13).

Those words have given me the thought and put the desire in my heart not to try to help those who do not need my help. Instead I must help those who need my help.

In Matthew 5:8, Jesus said, **"Blessed are the pure in heart: for they shall see God."**

He did not say, "Blessed are all the preachers and church members; they shall see God." He did not say, "Blessed are all the armies and navies that ever marched or sailed the seas; they shall see God." He did not say, "Blessed are all the kings that ever ruled, all the lawmakers, all the law explainers or interpreters, and all law enforcers; they shall see God." Jesus did not even say, "Blessed are they that have position, power, wealth and great fortune; they shall see God."

Jesus said, **"Blessed are the pure in heart: for they shall see God"** (Matthew 5:8).

Now then you know full well that without a pure heart we will not see God. Jesus made this so plain to us. A wayfaring man—no, even a fool—should not ere therein. If all the laws were taken from us and it was left to me to ask God for one law, I would ask for the law of love. If all the languages were taken from us but one language and I was to choose that language, I would choose the language of love.

Now then I want to talk to you in the following pages about life and the meaning of life. These topics have been the goal of human thought throughout all the ages. I will also discuss how to live and how to make an honest living. But I cannot do justice to all of these subjects in one little book when it would take seven books with a thousand pages or more to fully explore and expound these areas of human existence.

CHAPTER 3

A Child and Childish Behavior

A child, a baby, is God's most precious gift on God's green earth, a bundle of possibilities for good, regardless if they have been brought up, developed and trained to produce the abundant life. If lost from neglect or not used at all, this is part of a wasted life. God loved them, wanted them, needed them, would welcome them and could have used them, regardless if they were born in a mansion or in a log cabin, to a king or to a slave.

Of course, we often speak of people being fortunate and of some others more unfortunate than we are. We know full well it is a great blessing to be born in the stream of life that has been beautifully colored in the past with the pure in heart by living clean lives, with a sound mind, clean hands and a pure heart. A sterling character is good soil in which a beautiful soul can grow with health, character, intelligence and a willingness to work. Work will win, and faith will work wonders. To obey and keep the commands of God is a great and daring faith.

Jesus said the following words:

"Nevertheless, when the Son of man cometh, shall he find faith on the earth?" (Luke 18:8).

"Ye are my friends, if ye do whatsoever I command you" (John 15:14).

"If ye love me, keep my commandments" (John 14:15).

"Follow me, and I will make you fishers of men" (Matthew 4:19).

He did not say, "I will follow you, but you follow Me." On the other hand, there are those, we say, who are less fortunate. Sometimes I wonder if they are to blame as much as we blame them. There are those born in streams of life not only stirred up a little or made muddy but polluted with corruption by their ancestors' habits, works, deeds and lives, taking things into their lives they should have rejected and kept out of their lives, such as dope, whiskey, cigarettes and immoral living with all the diseases and effects it brings, too numerous to mention.

Without the care of mothers and others for babies and children it would be impossible for people to be living today. God bless our mothers with pure hearts and clean lives. What can equal the love of a mother's pure heart? To me, it is more like the love of Christ than anything I can think of, and I was never able to completely understand the love of Christ. Of course, we must admit we have some mothers, as well as some fathers, that do not have pure hearts. I have not been able to understand a mother who did not love her children as much as a mammy dog loved her pups under the floor. This goes, also, for a father who neglects his children.

Jesus said, **"Blessed are the pure in heart: for they shall see God"** (Matthew 5:8).

I say, "Cursed are the corrupt in heart, for they shall see the devil."

Praying mothers, what a blessing they are: Mothers praying before their babies are born and praying for their babies after they are born. God bless mothers who pray for their babies in the crib, holding their hands, before they can understand. And God bless mothers who hold their babies' hands in the cradle and pray for their babies after they can understand and read the Bible, thoughtfully, mindfully and prayerfully, with an open mind and an understanding heart; for in it is not only truth about God but a way of life He would have us to live to obtain eternal life.

Prayer: *We thank Thee, O God, for the Bible given us, for the wisdom to study diligently, for the lives of thy servants and for the teachings of thy servants, as recorded in the holy pages. Most of all we thank Thee for the life and message of Thy Son, Jesus. Amen.*

We must remember: A boy makes about the same kind of a man that he was a boy. Also, a girl makes about the same kind of a woman that she was a girl. These praying mothers are the greatest source for good on God's green earth. As little as we think about it, or as little as we care about it, it has made some of the greatest people around the world. In our own country it produced four preachers in one family, four medical doctors in another family, and four college presidents and one army general in another family. These are the high numbers, and the lower numbers are too numerous to mention.

I am talking to you from my memory and out of my own heart. I have known mothers who could not even read or write, not even their names. They just made a mark—X— and knew what it stood for. But they could pray, and they had faith. They knew how to work hard, tell the truth and live an honest, decent life. They too held the hands of their babies and prayed. I wish I could have heard them pray. I have tried to think of what might have been the words.

Could they have been something like the words in this prayer? *In the morning we thank Thee, our Father, for the past night's rest, the morning's blessings and this new day Thou hast given us. We thank Thee for all the blessings of life, the means of grace and the hope of glory. Amen.*

When we wake with the morning's light, it was God who kept us through the night. Then we raise our voices to God and pray:

O Lord, keep us through the day. Bless this baby. May it grow up to be a fine person in the world, one who will love Thee and serve and follow Thee. Keep him from sin during life. May he hunger and thirst after righteousness. Help children to do what is right and keep them from doing what is wrong. May they walk with Thee and please Thee. If they err, correct them. If they are weak, make them strong. If they fall, lift them up. If they sin, forgive them. Forgive them for each time they fail Thee. When they are bad, make them good. When they are ugly, make them nice. When they are dirty, make them clean. If they are filthy, make them pure, for in Jesus' mouth was found no guile. In Christ we pray. Amen.

CHAPTER 4

Big Things and Little Things

L ife is made up of so many, many little things, and the great majority of us will do only the little things in life. Those who have learned to do the little things well will have the opportunity to do something big and great in life. The little things in life are too numerous to mention, but let us take time to mention two or three of them, such as a pleasant smile, a kind word and a good deed.

We will start by examining a couple at the breakfast table. Now then a husband might say to his wife how much he loves her, how nice she looks, how wonderful she is, how much she means to him. He might tell her he could not live without her and even say, "I love you so. I would die for you." This is at breakfast.

Jesus said, **"Greater love hath no man than this, that a man lay down his life for his friends"** (John 15:13).

The same day at supper—called supper to me, but for people who are out of my class, it is called dinner—is a different picture. The husband might have had a hard day, or someone did him wrong, or when he got home his wife hurt his feelings. Perhaps she might have said the wrong thing at the wrong time. Now they are at the supper table, and the wife asks him to pass the biscuits, but he acts as if he did not hear. The husband will not pass the bread to her or even pass her the salt.

Now this is one example or a part of what I mean by "a child and childish things." To me, that husband is not grown up. He may be a man fifty years old and weigh two hundred pounds; but to me, he was acting — at that time — like a child. For him to die for his wife would have been a big thing, but to pass the bread or the salt would have been a little thing.

Were his words sincere? Were his acts, works, deeds and life — at that moment — pleasing to his wife and to God? I could go on and on, but this is a hint of what I mean — also what I mean by little things. Sometimes just a little turn in the right direction will send us on the road to health, happiness, success and heaven. On the other hand, just a little turn in the wrong direction will send us into the stream of sin, where we will be so quickly carried away in the swift current, dashed over its falls, broken in health, shattered in character and lost in hope.

Prayer: *Oh, Lord, our strength and our redeemer, may we not ask You to do for us what we can do for ourselves — for You know more and better what we need than we know to ask ourselves — but help us climb the steps of prayer into the light of faith and vision. Then, if we become inclined to peer anxiously into the future about the days yet to be, help us to know our time is in Your good hands. We have today, only this moment. May we live it well, that in the tomorrow we will have no regrets of the way we have lived today. Then goodness and mercy shall surely follow us all the days of our lives. Amen.*

This is a hint of what I will try to tell you about the good life later on from these written pages. It is hard to give what you do not have, but I will try, by the help of God, to give some of the best that is in me in a plain, simple way, as plain and as easy to understand and to read as I know how.

The Bible says, **"Train up a child in the way he should go: and when he is old, he will not depart from it"** (Proverbs 22:6).

Now that is good, but I say it would be better if the child would not depart from it while he was young, and I will tell you why I think so.

The Bible also says, **"Remember now thy Creator in the days of thy youth, while the evil days come not, nor the years draw nigh, when thou shalt say, I have no pleasure in them"** (Ecclesiastes 12:1).

That Bible also says, **"Honor thy father and thy mother: that thy days may be long upon the land that the Lord thy God giveth thee"** (Exodus 20:12).

This is a hint or stop sign printed, but later I will give you the red light to stop.

You cannot play with dogs without going away with fleas. You cannot run with the devil and walk with God. Birds of a feather will flock together. Life is made up with habits, whether they are good or whether they are bad. If you want potatoes, you must plant potatoes. If you want to have something when you are old, you should save something when you are young. I must say, there are more misers of lives than there are of money. If you keep the good life you will lose it. But if you give the good life you will save it.

Do we want to accumulate goods more than we want to accomplish good? Do we want God to listen to us more than we want to listen to God? Do we want to have our will more than we want God's will? Do we want to plan and plan and ask God to bless our plans and our ways, or do we want to say, *"Father, make us a blessing to Thy plan and to Thy way."*

If we listen, God will speak. If we will obey, God will command. To obey the commands of God is a great and daring faith. Work will win, and faith will work wonders. I think there are things that should be repeated, and you will hear some things repeated, hoping they will be remembered, used and indelibly impressed upon your mind.

CHAPTER 5

The World Offers Many Different Choices

The world offers many different choices. It is just as important to know what to reject and to keep out of our lives as it is to know what to accept and to take into our lives. This awareness, believed and lived, will beautifully color the stream of life—flowing down through the future time—with health, character, intelligence and a willingness to work.

Work will win, and faith will work wonders. **Faith** bids us to go forth into the unknown future, to face its problems, to undertake its tasks and to meet its emergencies. Faith is to ask God to take your hand and lead you through the storm. To me, **hope** is to be thankful for what has been done for us in the past, to be happy with the present time and to be hopeful of good things in the future. To me, **trust** is to be thankful we are children of the almighty God and He is our heavenly Father.

As we think is not what we might be, but it is what we are sure to become.

"Keep thy heart with all diligence; for out of it are the issues of life" (Proverbs 4:23).

The heart determines the saved life or the lost life, the good life or the wasted life.

Life is dangerous. It is full of little things and big things, good things and bad things. Life is a great servant, but a servant of what? Love is also a great servant, but a servant of what?

There is something in each and every one of us that can destroy us unless we possess a strict self-discipline with a sound mind, clean hands and a pure heart. That is why we all need Christ as our Savior. That is why God sent His beloved Son, as our master teacher, redeemer, Lord and Savior.

Children, let's relax. I am not a great thinker, nor am I a good writer either. I am not an expert at this. I am not scholarly. I am just a little barefooted country boy who could thin corn—my dad said, "Good"—but I have always wanted to serve God. I want to witness for Christ. God called me many years ago to try to teach people—girls and boys, women and men—to read the Bible and to pray. I answered that call. I have been trying, as best as I could, to witness for Christ from June 8, 1910. I do not mean to tell you in *The Plowboy* book of my adventures in this field or on this road of life all the teardrops and joys, the heartaches and the gladness, hungry and tired, weary and worn. I plan, if my life holds health, strength and mind, to write those adventures. I just mentioned the term "expert." I really do not desire to be an expert. Neither do I want an expert to try me, for he would hang me for sure.

Joke: *A friend of mine told me they had drilled a well for gas—on his father's land in the northeast corner of Clark County—over a thousand feet deep. The drilling company, he said, plugged the hole up, and you know what it was: Clark County all the way down.*

I feel that I have done about the same job of serving God as I did plowing corn for Dad. But I have faith and hope that God will fill my heart with joy someday when I hear Him say to me, "I did not know you could serve Me so well."

Prayer: *Our Father who art in heaven, teach us and make us teachable to the most beautiful things of life until we have wealth untold to share with others. Teach us how to pray and live as Thy children each day. Teach us to pray prayers we can help You to answer, for the good, beautiful and meaningful things, such as food, shelter, clothes, health, happiness, intelligence, character, a will to live and work, a desire to go about doing good. That was what Jesus did. He went about doing good, and in His mouth was found no guile. Now then give us strength and courage to labor for all these things that come from Thee and Thee alone. Amen.*

Now, children, not only does God love you, but I love you also. You see: God gives, but we receive. It is not a one-way street or a blind alley, not a dead-end road, as some people would have you believe. It is a two-way highway, a super highway, going and coming in both directions, giving and taking. Giving what and taking what? It is a two-way affair. Why do I know? Because Jesus said so, and to me, Jesus was full of grace and full of truth.

Our feet are the only feet here. Our hands are the only hands God has here. A pure heart is the only heart God has here. Let us give the best we have to God and to man. Keep to the right and watch out for the stop signs. Keep your hands upon the throttle and your eyes upon the rail, for life is like a mountain railroad. It is dangerous.

I will tell you about a few of the many dangers later on.

* PART TWO *

The Stream of Life, Beautifully Colored

If other nations do not pray for our nation, then I thank God if our nation will pray for other nations.

CHAPTER 6

Prayer and Growth

N ow, friends, when you pray prayers you can help God answer, you are coloring the stream of life beautifully. How and in what way? God hears and answers all prayers with either yes, no or wait a while.

A lot of times care, work, attention and other things go into this process of growth. We could mention a few: work, play, study, worship and love. These also are among the things that belong to God. With them we will live, and without them we will die. We are a part of all we come in contact with: food, shelter, clothes. All we eat and all we drink are a part of us. All we smell, see, feel, hear and taste. That is not all, and neither will I write them all down here for you to have. But I will go a little further to give what I think God wants you to have in order for you to be in that beautiful stream of life for which you have just prayed.

Now I want to lead you to Christ where He can help you to have the strength and courage to work and labor for those things. Let me say to you: Here is something you cannot see, hear, taste and smell. As for part of them, you have no control over them, have nothing to do with them and can do nothing about them. Those are the power, life, light and love of God.

Some of you might say, I don't believe one word of that. Well, I will mention two or three of them to you and will let you interpret the others yourself or think about them as you please. You probably will not agree with all I say anyway, for if I could be correct fifty-one percent of the time I would be the greatest person in the twentieth century.

What about a pain? Did you ever see one? Will you believe there is no pain because you cannot see it? You can feel it. You can't hear a pain. You can't see the wind, but you can feel it and hear it. You can't see a thought, but you can think. You cannot see the Holy Spirit, but you can feel it.

Jesus said, **"Howbeit when he, the Spirit of truth, is come, he will guide you into all truth: for he shall not speak of himself; but whatsoever he shall hear, that shall he speak: and he will shew you things to come"** (John 16:13). He did not say part of the truth; He said **"all truth."** Jesus was full of truth and full of grace.

Now, children, the Bible tells us, **"There is a way that seemeth right unto a man, but the end thereof are the ways of death"** (Proverbs 14:12).

Do we want to have our own way more than we want Jesus to have His way with us? Do we want Jesus to become more like us than we want to become like Jesus? What about what we eat and how we eat? Do we eat the proper kind of food: pure, good and wholesome? Not too much and not too little?

"And every man that striveth for the mastery is temperate in all things. Now they do it to obtain a corruptible crown; but we an incorruptible" (1 Corinthians 9:25).

Be temperate in all things: not too much and not too little, just the correct amount.

We could go on naming them, but is that necessary? You know them and how it works. You learn at home and at school about all that. The calories are fuel for the cells, and all the calories that are not burned are stored as fat. You have seen some people, no doubt, you thought were not overeating but who carry around extra weight, and that is hard on the heart. Anything we do to an excess will weaken the heart.

You can name them, from A to Z, from the cradle to the grave. What about dope, tranquilizers, whiskey, cigarettes, illicit sex, crime? The moral and spiritual life of our nation: This is just a part of it. You name it; it is there. The moral and spiritual life of our nation is a national disgrace. What is going on in our high schools and colleges? The spiritual and moral life of our nation is not only mildewed, worm-eaten and rat-bitten; it is decaying and filled with corruption. Smell it; it stinks. I have given you a hint. You name the others. They are there.

The Bible reads, **"The wicked shall be turned into hell, and all the nations that forget God"** (Psalm 9:17).

If I understand J. Edgar Hoover, former FBI director, correctly, he said we spend more money on crime in this country than we do on education and religion combined.

Is it possible we have too much religion and not enough salvation? But salvation and righteousness have become dirty words to some people. Some people are afraid of making others mad by teaching them about a heaven to gain and a hell to shun. As far as I am concerned, I love to give the devil a black eye. I don't have enough money and deceit to keep everybody speaking to me anyway. We are judged not only by our friends but by our enemies as well. I want to be on speaking terms with God and say a good word for Him always.

Talk about the high cost of living: A sinful life is the costliest life ever lived. The devil's big job is not only to discourage God's children, but he is on the job in a big way to slander God to man and to slander man to God and to one another. The devil is in the homes. He is in the churches. If the homes cannot get along, if the churches cannot get along, then for us to ask or expect the nations of the world to get along is a big order.

We have learned to do lots of things on the land, on the sea and in the air, but we have not learned how to live—how to gather, why, only one thing. We have not been teachable.

Jesus is more willing to draw us to Him than we are willing to come.

He is more willing to call us than we are willing to answer.

CHAPTER 7

The Kingdom of Christ

J esus is more willing to lead than we are to follow. He is more willing to teach than we are to learn. He is more willing to forgive than we are to repent. He is more willing to save the world than we are to let Him save us. He will do the saving, but surely we must do the letting.

"For God so loved the world, that he gave his only begotten Son, that whosoever believeth in him should not perish, but have everlasting life" (John 3:16).

That is good, but it would be better if we could say the world so loved God that they received His gift. Then we would not know this old world. That is the great need today. There is enough to turn the kingdom of this world into the kingdom of Christ.

What is the kingdom of Christ? The kingdom of Christ, the kingdom of God and the kingdom of heaven are all the same. It is more, but it is not less, than happiness, righteousness, joy, peace, love and service. The Holy Spirit will lead us in the ways of all truth, not part, but I say all. That, and only that, will make it safe for our mothers, our sisters, our wives, our daughters, our granddaughters and our great-granddaughters. As long as the Lord our God shall call, love is the answer. I mean to tell you more about this in "The Meaning of Life."

Let's get our breath. I'm not as smart perhaps as you are, but, really, this is hard for a fellow like me with a single-track mind and only one talent to think with. It sometimes puts me in a dream. I can be spoken to and can't hear the speaker. It is harder for me to write this than it will be for you to read it.

The tears that have been shed and the prayers that have been prayed to write this will never, no, never, be repeated by the ones who read it—that is, if it is ever read. Perhaps it will be thrown in the wastebasket (so often referred to by railroad office men as "file thirteen"), put in the fireplace and burned or taken to a little brown building in the country just big enough for one or two and used as a Sears Roebuck catalogue would be used.

Then, I must say, they are wading through the tears I have shed for them and the prayers I have prayed for them and are going on down to a devil's hell. I would rather be a convict than to be a girl or a boy, a woman or a man, who would wade through the tears and prayers that were prayed for me. It wouldn't matter if it was a mother, a father, a brother or a sister, an aunt or an uncle, a nephew or a niece, a grandfather or a grandmother, a preacher or a teacher or a child of God anywhere, anytime and anyplace.

Joke. This reminds me of the good old lady who went to church so regularly and faithfully. The preacher was condemning sin by name, and she enjoyed it so much. When he would say "drinking whiskey," the good old lady would nudge, with her elbow, the lady sitting next to her and say, "That is preaching." Dope, not telling the truth, being dishonest, smoking cigarettes, wrong things, every indulgence—too many to mention them all—she would go ahead with the same procedure and saying each time, "Now that is preaching." At last, and by no means the least to her, the preacher spoke out against using snuff. She then nudged or elbowed her seatmate for the last time with these words, "Look out! He has quit preaching and gone to meddling."

Prayer: *Our Father and our God, You know our needs. You hear our calls and are abundantly answering our prayers. Fill us with perfect faith and trust in Thee. We are thankful Thou did send this Savior of mankind into the world, into this earth, to reveal Thy loving heart to us and Thy concern for us, not only to know more about Him but to become more like Him, through song, sermon, meditation and prayer. May our works, deeds and lives speak of His love and mercy, His light and truth, His devotion and faith, and last but by no means least to speak of His righteousness and salvation. May we be kind and gentle to those who are old, for kindness and gentleness are better than gold. We are workers together, whosoever will, none left out. God wants, loves, needs and can use all that have ever been born or all that will ever be born to make the words of Jesus come true: Thy kingdom come.*

You already know what the kingdom of God is: Thy will be done on earth. That is where you and I are today. What is God's will? God is not willing that any should perish but all should come to repentance. What is repentance? It is more than—but it is not less than—a change of direction and a change of mind. But repentance is also a change of words, works, deeds and lives with hearts pure and souls honest, full of truth and full of grace.

CHAPTER 8

The Nature and Nurture of Children

This growth of a baby, a child and our teenagers is a wonderful period, an important period. It is thrilling to watch them grow—physically, mentally, morally, emotionally and spiritually—all in need of attention, cultivation and care. Growing depends on more, much more, than the sower, the seed or grain, and the soil being well prepared.

What I have tried so hard to do is to pray—through tear-dimmed eyes and with a heart filled with loving prayers—for all mankind everywhere around the world, this side of the iron curtain or behind the iron curtain or any other curtain that separates them from God. His love and care for mankind are so watchful.

Regarding our children, I am thinking of the environment and cultivation in which they live and grow, in comparison to the soil of the good earth. What kind of soil is it? Is it good, deep, fertile soil that lays well? Can we do our part, or have we done our part? Is there any earthly way to increase the fertility of this soil so we can have an abundant harvest?

I wish I could sing an old, familiar church hymn to you in this deep baritone voice of mine—if you would enjoy listening to it as much as I would enjoy singing it to you or if it would move you as much as it moves me.

Children, bless your hearts. It is hard to give you what I do not have, but I am giving you some of the best that is in me with this little single-track mind. I am using it for traffic in both directions, eastbound and westbound traffic.

If we will listen, God will speak; and if we will obey, God will command.

Prayer: *O God, with myself I can do nothing, but with Christ I can master, conquer and accomplish things through Him who strengthens me. Take my hands, precious Lord, and lead me on. Amen.*

Now then we haven't left that cornfield. We are still in there, thinning corn, plowing and hoeing. It is in the knobs rolling and not in the best of soil, but we will have to do the best with what we have at the time and place. It is not ready to lay by, and I do not have time to go to the shade. But I will take a drink of good, fresh water from the old spout spring down there in the cool shade, out of this gourd I raised by myself. It will hold about two pints. It has a straight handle on it, about eighteen to twenty inches long. I made a drinking gourd out of it by taking my knife and cutting a hole about three inches in diameter or four inches, getting the seeds and pulp out. That makes a nice drinking gourd. This is a good drink of water. It tastes good to a dry and thirsty mouth and throat. Now I am not leaving you to go to the shade or lay you by.

A child gets his finger hurt, and the mother kisses it. Sometimes that helps, especially with that pretty smile and those kind, soothing words—not too much scolding and fussing—but in a home where children feel they are loved and wanted. That is a blessing that makes them happy. They learn also by doing. Parents make them feel they are useful and helpful and that the parents would have a hard time getting along without those children. Good, healthy girls and boys can live clean lives with strong, healthy bodies and minds by keeping their clothes clean, their hands clean, their minds clean, their hearts clean, their bodies clean and their homes clean. These kinds of children are the finest investment in the world.

A boy makes about the same kind of a man that he is a boy; a girl makes about the same kind of a woman that she is a girl. Of course, life is a dangerous thing, not only from heredity and environment. There are a thousand and one things that can harm a person: accidents, diseases and bad habits. The good things, such as good food, people should take into their bodies and lives.

On the other hand, all the bad habits and things too numerous to mention, all wrong things, will muddy the stream of life that will flow down through the stream of time. The descendant of a habitual drunkard, medical science indicates, goes to the tenth generation and causes damages that will affect the minds and bodies of future generations. Drunkards harm the stream of life by making it so muddy and ugly that it makes me cry to even think of them, much less name all the misery, heartaches and wasted lives. I find myself crying from the depth of my soul for some of them I have known or known about.

God bless our precious boys and girls, the finest God could give us, from all His laws of nature. However, those boys and girls have been affected by how their fathers and mothers have kept God's laws or have broken those laws, in ways that are physical, mental, moral, emotional and spiritual. Sometimes, I think, from the bottom of my heart—with what a small, limited mind I have—we can blame nothing on our boys and girls. They did not ask to come into this world. They had no part or choice in this physical birth. But they will have a part and a choice in the spiritual birth or second birth I will tell you about in another chapter.

"Jesus answered and said unto him, Verily, verily, I say unto thee, Except a man be born again, he cannot see the kingdom of God" (John 3:3).

The Bible does not say "some," but it says all "whosoever will." Children could not say who would be their mother and father, what nation, race or color, a boy or a girl, red-headed or black headed, blue eyes or brown eyes, tall or short, fat or lean, wise or foolish, strong or weak, sickly or well, laughing or crying, cursing or praying.

Bless their precious hearts. They could not say if they would be born in a clean house or a dirty house, in a mansion or in a stable, in a bed or on a pile of hay, straw or fodder on the ground. They could not say if their parents would be healthy or sickly, strong or weak, intelligent or ignorant, good or bad, rich or poor, a liar or a thief, a saint or a sinner. Are they responsible if they do not have food, shelter or clothes?

CHAPTER 9

Second Birth: Spiritual Birth

If children are not well fed and nurtured, it will eventually make a difference to society. If they are starved—physically, mentally, morally, emotionally and spiritually—this will affect society. If they are well provided for with the blessings of life—namely food, shelter, clothes, good homes, good parents, properly cared for, trained, educated, not leaving out the moral and spiritual life—it makes a difference to society.

The moral and spiritual life of our nation today is decaying. With tear-dimmed eyes this day I bow my head in shame that I have not done a better job for our precious boys and girls or had a part in making such a mess of things for you. This is a part of one reason why my soul is crying out to girls and boys, women and men, here and everywhere.

"For God so loved the world, that he gave his only begotten Son, that whosoever believeth in him should not perish, but have everlasting life" (John 3:16).

That is good. That is safe. That is beautiful. The sad part of it is that we cannot say all the people in the world have so loved God, received that gift, believed and been baptized in the name of Christ, saying in their hearts, "Christ is the Son of God, and I accept Him as my Savior." That is what produces the second birth, the spiritual birth, when it is done with an honest, pure heart. That is what gives you the power to become a child of God. The spirit of God will lead you in the ways of all truth, for you have from that moment begun to live forever. That is eternal life. When we are dealing with truth we are dealing with eternal life.

Life is a great servant: a servant of what? Love is a great servant: a servant of what? What kind of life do we live or what do we love? There is a heaven to gain and a hell to shun. That is the only choice we have. Which will it be for you? I wish I could see all men everywhere respond to that calling: the lost ones saved and the saved ones strengthened.

Then and only then will the words of Jesus come true when He said, **"Thy kingdom come. Thy will be done in earth, as it is in heaven"** (Matthew 6:10). Then we would see the kingdom of this world turned into the kingdom of Christ.

For what can we blame our boys and girls? (I will tell you later.) What are they except what we have given them, taught them, trained them, said or left unsaid, done or left undone? Have we given them things from God, or have we given them things from the devil? If we had a gift from God, would we give it to boys and girls, or would we give it to men and women? Would we just keep it? If we just keep it we will lose it; but if we give it we will save it. For when we are dealing with youth we are dealing with eternity. Is it what we have done for our children, or is it what we have done to them? Now I am not talking about food, shelter, clothes, a fine car to drive (that is something I will talk about later when we get in the danger zone on life's highway), gold and silver, a big bank account. I will let you name the others, but this is a hint.

If you do not remember anything I have said or will say later, here is one of a few things. I will try not to talk too much or mention too many things that will confuse your minds, or you will not remember any of them at all.

Important topics: *Let the following words be impressed upon your minds indelibly:* **health, intelligence, character** *and* **a willingness to work.**

This goes back a thousand years into the past, and this is not any too soon to begin to prepare and train a child, as I see it. It can, when applied to a child, beautifully color the stream of life that will flow down through the future time for a thousand years, kept clean with a pure heart by each generation.

I think Christ meant more, but not less, than this when He said, **"Blessed are the pure in heart: for they shall see God"** (Matthew 5:8).

I say, Cursed are the corrupt in heart, for they shall see — with all their immoral, corrupt sin and evil hearts — the devil. Now then what about those that have corrupted the stream of life, those who will never receive Christ as their Savior? Is that what they have done for our children or what they have done to our children?

Although I do not have all the answers — for the unknown is greater than the known — it is the will of human beings (is it not?), even the will of the smartest and the best. Let us not worry too much about what man has done to us; we cannot do anything about that. But be thankful for what God has done for us or for what He can do for us. Do something about that and know the difference. The world offers so many different things.

Prayer: *Help us, O God, to know what to keep out and what to take in and use. Amen.*

What have people — the home, church, school, radio, television, movies and press — taught our children? We will get out of them just about what we put in. That is all, for we are a part of all we have inherited and of our environment. We are influenced by all we have learned, through all sources, all habits. We are affected by all things we have taken into our bodies or our lives to use — whether they are good or bad. Life is made up of habits: good or bad. Yes, children have a responsibility to obey their parents and to love them, to work and to help in all things, to do what is right, to share the work and to share with the work.

Now then, children, up to this time, I have tried to say what I thought God wanted me to say to you and to your parents. We have worked hard to clean and clear the ground of briars, bushes and weeds. If there were any gullies in the field, fill them with what we had cleaned and cleared from the ground, weigh them down with rocks, with dirt from each side of the gullies, so the ground is clean and smooth.

Now we will plow the field for corn, this year's crop. We will harrow, roll and lay off in corn rows about three feet wide. Now we are ready to plant and fertilize. We have our soil well prepared and cleaned, and it looks like good soil, pure soil.

Important: A *sterling character is good soil in which to grow a beautiful soul.*

Now my recollection about this cornfield, when I was a boy, was a field fenced with an old-fashioned wood-rail fence, laid crooked. Perhaps the ground rail, or worm rail, was laid on a rock at the corner or each panel placed at about a ten-percent angle left and then the next rail set at about ten percent to the right, and so on, on a straight line as far as you wanted to fence. Some of the fences extended on a long stretch, running for miles and miles, especially along the county roads, dirt roads. That was all we had when I was a boy, with horses and wagons for the lower-class people and horses and buggies for the upper-class people—often referred to as the poor and the rich. Many of those county roads are super highways now.

We want to keep in mind a few of the many things in this business of raising a field, whether it be of corn, wheat, oats, rye, clover, grass or red cane for a real good sweet sorghum molasses—all the other things from the good earth. Many things are necessary in order to be successful: the planter or sower, the seed or grain, the soil, the workers and the reaper.

Although the times were a lot different back then from what they are now, the moral and spiritual life of a person, nevertheless, should still be clean, honest and pure today as then. My boyhood has been not only days and days ago or months and months ago but years and years ago. Some are old at forty, and some are young at seventy. I do not feel old.

"I have been young, and now am old; yet have I not seen the righteous forsaken, nor his seed begging bread" (Psalms 37:25).

Now then, children, I have stood by you and made it plain to you and for you that you could not help how you came into this world. But by the Spirit of God, by the Spirit of Christ, you can help what you do after you are here and have reached the age of accountability.

* PART THREE *

Many Dangers: In Life and in Death

*For God so loved mankind that He gave His Son for all;
but all of mankind has not so loved God that they have
received His gift of light, life, truth, grace and love.*

CHAPTER 10

A Few of the Many Dangers

Children, do you want your parents to obey you more than you want to obey your parents? Do you want your parents to follow you more than you want to follow your parents? Do we want God to obey us more than we want to obey God? Do we want God to follow us more than we want to follow God? Do we want to tell our parents what to do more than we want our parents to tell us what to do? Do we want to tell God what to do more than we want God to tell us what to do? Do we want our parents to be on our side more than we want to be on God's side? If we are on God's side, we will win.

Let's take courage and fight for sound minds, clean hands and an honest, pure heart, for health, intelligence, character and a willingness to work, by keeping our minds clean, our eyes clean, our mouths clean—for in Jesus' mouth was found no guile—and our ears clean.

"Who did no sin, neither was guile found in his mouth" (1 Peter 2:22).

In my day a popular derogatory expression was "You are a fool" instead of "You are a square." Other terms of derision were "coward" or "chicken," but it is all the same. That is what mockers will say to you today. Who are they? I will make it plain. The children of the devil will tell you that you are a chicken or you are a square if you don't do this bad thing or if you don't do that bad thing. But that is not the truth. The truth is that you will be foolish if you do it. Keep your hands clean, your body clean, your clothes clean, your home clean, for God does not dwell in an unclean person, place or thing.

The apostle Paul said, **"What? Know ye not that your body is the temple of the Holy Ghost which is in you, which ye have of God, and ye are not your own"** (1 Corinthians 6:19).

If you will let Him, Christ will come in, but you will have to do the letting. You will have to do the inviting. He will not force His way in. He will not shoot His way in. With Christ you are everything, and you can do all things; but without Him you are nothing, and you can do nothing. Christ is our sufficiency with nothing left out; it is all there.

Do you want to tell your parents where you are going, or do you want your parents to tell you where to go? Do you want to tell your parents when you are coming back if you tell them at all? Do you want your parents to tell you when to come back? I recollect, across the years, many that did not come back. Should we watch our company and the company we keep, the places we go, the things we do, the things we say?

It is dangerous not to hunger and thirst after righteousness. We have to want to do right and to be something. It is dangerous not to obey the commands at home, the commands at school and the commands of God. We can go too fast; if we go a little slower and proceed more cautiously, we may be surer of getting to our destination and living longer. If we knew where we were going, we might not be in such a hurry anyway.

Joke: *Two dogs were watching a bunch of teenagers doing the twist on television. One dog said to the other dog, "Now what do you think of that?" The other dog replied, "Well, when I act like that, they give me flea powder."*

Stir up the gift that is within you. Just be yourself. If my life, mind and body hold out and endure, the next book I plan to write will be *The Mill Boy*.

In this book, *The Plowboy*, we are working in the cornfield and comparing that to boys and girls, men and women. We are looking not only at their words but also at their works, their deeds and their lives. We are exploring what it takes to produce a field of corn: toil and sweat, sometimes with blood and tears, and sometimes the workers are hungry and thirsty, tired, weary and worn. We are examining the significance of sunshine, rain, soil and grain. Just how much work does it take after the corn is planted? How dangerous would it be not to thin corn, not to plow the corn, not to hoe the corn and not to keep the weeds out? Even after we cleaned the ground, plowed it and planted it the field is, by no means, through requiring attention, care and cultivation. If the cornfield was turned loose, not plowed, thinned and hoed, where would it be?

Of course, we have solely to depend on God for the air, rain and sunshine. We do not work or pay money for the freshness of the air, the sunshine and the rain. If God would take just one of them from us, where would we be? Therefore, you see, we do not pay for some things that are worth more to us than things for which we do pay money. Gold and silver will wear away, but the Spirit of Christ—as well as the good things our parents and others have put in our hearts—will never decay.

How about you and me and others? Will we do as well, or will we do as ill, in giving this spirit? If we have it and give it we will save it. If we keep it we will lose it. We owe as much to the next generation and more to make the progress we should in this changing world. To meet our obligations and responsibilities, just as much as was required of our parents to give us, we must also encourage the next generations to have strong, healthy, intelligent, clean and pure bodies with character and a willingness to work.

Remember: *A sterling character is good soil in which a beautiful soul can grow. Work will win, and faith will work wonders.*

We have not all been fortunate in our inheritance from heredity and environment. No. Will all of us have that storehouse of wealth from God and man to give to others here and now and to pass on to others? Our boys and girls today will be our men and women tomorrow. The kind of boys and girls today will greatly determine what kind of men and women we will have tomorrow. Of course there are exceptions, but I am speaking as a general rule or as they might be classified.

Now, fathers and mothers, boys and girls, men and women, in the human field of life toil, sweat, blood and tears are also required, not only hungering and thirsting after righteousness and salvation. God's love and ever presence give us comfort, peace, light and truth, which is food for our souls. This is also in great demand for all people everywhere but more especially for all children everywhere as they grow in stature and in favor with God and man. Our young people should grow in the good, beautiful and meaningful things of life with all the good education they can take or can be given.

If they cannot be great, we pray they will be good, useful, self-supporting citizens who know how to live and how to make a living, going about doing good and expecting a lot of themselves but expecting a little from the other fellow.

Anyone who loves God and will keep His commandments, to me, is a good and great person.

CHAPTER 11

If We Do or If We Fail to Do

*Neither do men light a candle, and put it
under a bushel, but on a candlestick; and it
giveth light unto all that are in the house.
(Matthew 5:15)*

To teach is one thing and is good, but to be teachable is another thing and is better. It is a dangerous thing for us to fail to ask God to teach us how to become richer in the most beautiful things of life so that we have wealth untold to share with others.

The home, the church, the school—how important all this is, laboring together in one bundle of love, to produce this harvest. The credit for producing good and successful young people goes to all three. On the other hand, if a generation of young people has gone astray, society must not put blame on just one of these areas but on all.

I put the foremost importance on "the home" for the success or failure of our children. Of course there are exceptions in all cases. I will not say no, not by any means. I am solely speaking for myself and no one else. I will take the blame for what I am saying and blame no one else if I am wrong. So many times I say I was wrong. If I could be right fifty-one percent of the time, I would be the greatest figure in the twentieth century.

All the best people and all the saints do not come from the rich homes, but I do not say all the failures in life and all the sinners in life come from the poor homes. The homes that can well provide the necessary things for children, particularly a good education, should be a blessing to them. But I can recollect where it seemed to me to be a curse or a downfall. On the other hand, I have seen poor homes (if you want to measure in worldly goods) produce bright and gifted children with strong, healthy bodies and minds; I have seen their children to be honest, clean and pure, with a will to work and a will to win.

I realize full well that I am glad I was born at the bottom of the ladder of success and education because I had nothing to do but climb. Work will win, and faith will work wonders. I will do my part. I would rather be at the bottom and go up than to be at the top and come down. I could go on and on and name you a lot of comparisons, but this is a hint I have given you regarding many things. Now here is the football; make them a touchdown. That is what they want of you, and that is what they are expecting of you. Take it and go.

Important: *Do not ask for a lighter load in life but ask God to help you to be strong in order to carry this heavy load that life affords, realizing full well it is less vital what happens to you than what you allow the happenings to do to you. Do not ask God or anyone else to do for you the things you can do for yourself.*

This is an individual affair. Are you like this? Are you like the little boy who said, "Mother, I am going to say my prayers, so is there anything you want?"

If you are not doing for yourself, I would ask you to repent. The word "repent" means to change. Some people say "to change the mind," but it means a lot more to me than just the mind. To me it means much more, but not less, than direction, heart, habits, desires, thirst and soul. You can name the others since I am trying to get you in the habit of thinking and contemplating these matters. I am writing to you or talking to you from the printed pages of my heart. It is so hard for a person to give what he or she does not have. Could that be the case? Are you perhaps getting so little because I had so little to give?

Reflection: *As the clock ticks the time away here on the wall, I am just taking one step at a time, not knowing what I am going to say. When I get through I wonder if you will know what I have said, if I have said anything worthwhile, if it is of God, ever so small.*

We can clear the field, plow the soil and plant the seed. You are the harvest.

Will it be a good harvest of good fruit? Will it be? It all does not depend on the sower, the seed and the soil. There is also a part for you to play. How will you use what you have been given? What kind of soil are the seeds planted in? Of course it also requires work, care and attention. The weeds will grow if the field is neglected. The farmer can sit in the shade, but the weeds will grow. Of course there is no harm in sitting in the shade, but if you sit in the shade all the time where would you be? What kind of shape will the field be in?

How do you spend your leisure time, such as thirty minutes a day, for one year? If you are just an average reader, you can read the New Testament through six times and get understanding, for things are not as they may seem. Even your eyes may deceive you. Sometimes in life it has been hard for me to believe what I saw or what I heard.

Anecdote: *One of the many things along this line was an old stub standing. The birds had a nest, or the yellow hammers had drilled two holes in there and built their nests. One day I was watching the birds flying up and going in one at a time. A bird would go in the bottom hole and, I assumed, out of the top and fly away. I thought, I can't tell if that bird is going in at the hole it is supposed to go in or if it is coming out at the hole it is supposed to come out. Suddenly out popped the other bird, and then I understood there were two separate birds with two separate nests of young they were feeding.*

CHAPTER 12

The Leaving Spirit And the Dangerous Road

There is a different way of life now than when I was a boy, but risk and danger still exist. Life is more dangerous now, and there are more people. Then we had dangers, such as birds of the air and varmints of the woods to damage our crops. Other dangers included rattlesnakes and copperhead snakes, kicking mules and kicking horses, and the possibility of a timber falling on people and things.

The *leaving spirit* of the prodigal son was also dangerous. Do we not have a great amount of that spirit in us? Do we often say, "Give me; give me," instead of saying, "Thank you; thank you"? Do we say, "Give me wealth that we might go out in the world and waste it," or "Give me health that I might go out in the world and destroy it"?

Can we see ourselves as we are and say, **"I will arise and go to my father, and will say unto him, Father, I have sinned against heaven, and before thee, and am no more worthy to be called thy son: make me as one of thy hired servants"** (Luke 15:18-19)?

May we not plan and plan and ask God to bless our plans and ways, but may we ask our Father to make us a blessing to

His plan and His way? Can we stand a little success without losing our heads? Can we take a little disappointment without becoming a failure in life? It is bad for children to disobey their parents, but it is worse for us to grieve God.

"Be ye therefore ready also: for the Son of man cometh at an hour when ye think not" (Luke 12:40).

If we do not believe in the Word, God can get along without us, but we cannot get along without God. We are on a *dangerous road*. If we sing the song "I Will Follow Thee Always" but turn off at the first pig path, that is dangerous. If we feel Him draw near but do not come, if we hear Him call and do not answer, if we see Him leading but do not follow, if we hear Him teach but refuse to learn, if we hear Him forgiving but will not repent, if we see and hear Him saving but will not let Him save us—then we are on a dangerous road.

Jesus said, **"And I, if I be lifted up from the earth, will draw all men unto me"** (John 12:32).

He did not say, as I have heard quoted many times in my life, "If I be lifted up from the earth, all men will come unto me." There is a difference in being "drawn" and "coming." There is also a difference in being called and answering.

Your mother may say, "Come here," or "Come here, Mary." You heard her, but you did not necessarily answer her. You probably did not even go to her call. You know the difference and why. Did you want to have your way more than you wanted your mother to have her way? Did you want to play more than you wanted to help your mother or father do what they wanted you to do? Did you want your will to be done more than you wanted your mother's or father's will to be done? Now then you know the difference and know what you did about it.

But if you heard the call, answered, went and obeyed the command, blessed are you. On the other hand, if you heard but did not answer, did not go and did not obey the command, then you know why. Could it have been because you did not want to? Was it stubbornness? Was it laziness? Was it because your parents might want you to peel potatoes or go and get a bucket of water? You know. I do not.

It has been a long time since I was a boy, and I am talking in terms of that day. Times are so different, but if we do not have responsibilities and work now, then we surely should have them. We do have a lot of wonderful boys and girls, trying hard and working hard, but I am suggesting, in other words, this thought:

Whoever disobeys God and Christ and whosoever disobeys parents, teachers or the preacher—the home, the school, the church—and teaches others to do so will be the least in the kingdom of Christ.

All children of God around the world should try—with all of their human flesh, mind, soul and body—to turn the kingdom of this world into the kingdom of Christ. All those who keep God's commandments and do them and who teach others to do so will be called the greatest in the kingdom of Christ.

When **"one of his disciples said unto him, Lord, teach us how to pray"** (Luke 11:1), a few of Jesus' words were these: **"Thy kingdom come. Thy will be done, as in heaven, so in earth"** (Luke 11:2).

God's will is not that any should perish but that all should come to repentance. God wants you to be in that number. Do you want to be in that number? What am I doing, what are you doing, to help every child around this world turn the kingdom of this world into the kingdom of Christ?

Producing a field of corn, grass, clover or wheat requires toil, sweat and work. In order to reap the harvest, the laborer must plow, hoe and thin the crop to eliminate the weeds that will grow if the crop is neglected. This is the same process to produce the good, fruitful things for the nourishment of our bodies. Likewise, to produce a great harvest for the kingdom of Christ here on earth also takes great care, service and attention as we turn the kingdom of this world into the kingdom of Christ.

The kingdom of Christ is more than, but is not less than, happiness, righteousness, joy, peace, love and service in the Holy Spirit—all of which will keep the mind clean, the body clean, the clothes clean and the home clean with an honest, clean, pure heart.

Prayer: *God, bless Christians all around the world. Shield and defend them from the evil intentions of their enemies, only as Thou knowest how. Amen.*

* PART FOUR *

THE GREAT THEME

With Jesus we will live, but without Him we will die.

Jesus is not only the light and hope of the world but the life and resurrection. With Him we will live, but without Him we will die.

P. M. Williams with his children:
Norman, Rudolph, Sarah and Hubert

CHAPTER 13

Come, Follow, Tarry and Go

Joke: Uncle Bill planted a potato patch, and it was fine. That fall when he was digging his Irish potatoes Uncle Joe passed by and asked Uncle Bill, "How did your taters turn out?" Uncle Bill said, "By guineas, they did not turn out because the old sow got in and rutted them out."

> **Prayer:** *Our Father who art in heaven, You know our needs, You hear our calls, and You are abundantly answering our prayers. You hear and answer all prayers with either yes, no or wait a while. Fill us with perfect trust in Thee. Save the lost and strengthen the saved. In Christ we pray. Amen.*

Friends, you have been listening to my words, and I thank you for your good and kind attention. My words are small potatoes to be compared or weighed with the words of Jesus. Now listen to the words of the good and great teacher Jesus, and as we repeat those old and familiar words may God give us a new and deeper meaning.

Jesus said to come, to tarry and to go. **"*Come* unto me, all ye that labour and are heavy laden, and I will give you rest"** (Matthew 11:28). **"Behold, I send the promise of my Father upon you: but *tarry* ye in the city of Jerusalem,** until ye be endued with power from on high" (Luke 24:49). *"Go* ye therefore, and teach all nations, baptizing them in the name of the Father, and of the Son, and of the Holy Ghost: teaching them to observe all things whatsoever I have commanded you: and, lo, I am with you always, even unto the end of the world. Amen" (Matthew 28:20).

How short, plain and simple these words are: come, tarry and go. Could you or I use such plain simple words to mean so much? Now let us see what other great truths Jesus said. He says what He means, and He means what He says.

"Then said Jesus unto his disciples, If any man will come after me, let him deny himself, take up his cross, and follow me" (Matthew 16:24).

"And he saith unto them, Follow me, and I will make you fishers of men" (Matthew 4:19).

"Ye are my friends, if ye do whatsoever I command you" (John 15:14).

"If ye love me, keep my commandments" (John 14:15).

"This is my commandment, That ye love one another, as I have loved you" (John 15:12).

Jesus also said, in effect, "Now you are fitted, filled and well prepared for My command." Go into all the world, teaching all things He has taught you to go about doing good. Give all things He has given you. Do not say they are yours and keep them. If you do you will lose them; but if you will give them you will save them. Remember and say they were given to you by Jesus, and you must share them with the world.

This is the seed that will fall in the clean, honest, pure heart to bring the harvest of the abundant life, overflowing, and He will be with you always to the end of the world. Jesus did not say part of the time; He said all the time. Jesus did not say part of the way; He said all the way. Jesus will save us according to the promises of His Word.

We could not take the words **come, follow, tarry** and **go** and make very much out of them. But you see clearly what Christ could do with the little things when He got through by adding His blessing to it. I believe with all my heart that love through Christ is the answer to the individual and to the world. I mean to tell you more about it in a few pages ahead. The individual will never be any better than the Spirit of Christ in him.

Making a long leap to keep from talking so much, I will let you think a little as I hope you will. This is a hint, and the wise person needs only a hint. Here is the basketball. Take it, and make us a goal. That is what we want.

The home will never be any better than the individuals within it, and the world will never be any better than the individuals who make it up—whether they are good or bad, wise or foolish, sick or well, diseased or whole, strong or weak, old or young (some are old at forty, and some are young at eighty), truthful or false, a liar or a thief, a saint or a sinner.

We are all sinners: either a saved sinner or a lost sinner. That is why Jesus said, **"But go ye and learn what that meaneth, I will have mercy, and not sacrifice: for I am not come to call the righteous, but sinners to repentance"** (Matthew 9:13).

Jesus wanted to change their minds because He wanted to call the sinner to repentance. He wanted to change each sinner's mind, heart and soul to take him off the road to death and destruction and to follow Him. Jesus said in effect, "I know the way, but you do not. Let me show you the way to eternal life."

"Jesus said unto her, I am the resurrection, and the life; he that believeth in me, though he were dead, yet

shall he live: And whosoever liveth and believeth in me
shall never die. Believest thou this?" (John 11:25-26).

To live is Christ. To get out of this body of flesh, or to
die, is gain. It is just a change of address for every child of
God, but it is a beautiful change.

"For to me to live is Christ, and to die is gain"
(Philippians 1:21).

In Christ was God, reconciling the world unto Himself,
a perfect God in man and a perfect man in God. God knew
there was something in all people that would destroy them,
even though He made them in His own image.

Genesis 1:28-29 reads, "And God said, Let us make
man in our image, after our likeness: and let them have
dominion over the fish of the sea, and over the fowl of the
air, and over the cattle, and over all the earth, and over
every creeping thing that creepeth upon the earth. So
God created man in his own image, in the image of God
created he him; male and female created he them."

That is why God sent His beloved Son into the world to
be our Savior. We know Him as our teacher, but do we know
Him as our Savior? The life and message of Jesus will affect
our lives, not only in words, but also in works and deeds.
Sure as we live, we can strive to turn the kingdoms of this
world into the kingdom of Christ.

Jesus instructed the disciples in this manner: "And as
ye go, preach, saying, The kingdom of heaven is at hand.
Heal the sick, cleanse the lepers, raise the dead, cast out
devils: freely ye have received, freely give" (Matthew
10:7-8).

If the kingdoms of this world become the kingdom of
Christ, that will be the answer of all those lessons teachers
have taught, all those sermons preachers have preached, all
those songs choirs have sung and all the prayers people have
prayed. Where will the jails and penitentiaries be? Where
would our hospitals and asylums be? If the good life could

do away with half of them, I would rather live there than here now. You talk about the high cost of living. A sinful life is the costliest life that was ever lived. A wasted life is gone with no good to himself, his fellow man or God.

CHAPTER 14

Faith: The Power of Salvation

The Bible speaks of violence on earth in the last days. Can we see any signs of that today? I will take the time to tell you or to call it by name. I could not tell you anything you do not know. Have I told you anything you do not already know? Probably I only called to your attention things you already know. It would not only please every child of God around the world, but it would please God to see all of His creation be born again and receive His gift in faith.

"For God so loved the world, that he gave his only begotten Son, that whosoever believeth in him should not perish, but have everlasting life" (John 3:16).

Faith to the lost is foolishness; but to the saved it is the power of God unto salvation. All those jails and pens are full of religion, but they are not full of righteousness and salvation. If the lost would let Jesus save them, we would not know this old world. Jesus will save them, but they have got to do the letting.

Jesus is more willing to draw them than they are willing to come. He is more willing to call them than they are to answer. He is more willing to lead them than they are willing to follow. He is more willing to teach than they are to learn. He is more willing to forgive them than they are willing to repent. He is more willing to save the world than the world is willing to let Him save them.

If the lost people would allow Jesus into their hearts, we could then turn those jails and pens into homes for the poor and needy, for old folks, for little children who have no homes and for those children no one wants. Some of them are gifted. If those gifted children only had the opportunity, they would shake this old world with the power they have in them.

The Bible says the wicked will be turned into hell and the nations that forget God will perish. If all the lessons they ever heard taught, all the sermons they ever heard preached, all the songs they ever heard sung and all the prayers they ever heard prayed will never bring them to God, there is one thing that will bring them to God, and that is the judgment.

Prayer: *Dear God, save the lost and strengthen the saved. Amen.*

If all men everywhere would be filled with truth and grace, with love and mercy, and if all people around the earth would be filled with the life and message of Christ, then this world could be a safe place for all people everywhere: our mothers, our sisters, our wives, our daughters, our grand-daughters, our great-granddaughters, and on and on.

Prayer: *I pray, O God, for the life and message of Christ to ring out from the homes, from the pulpits and from the classrooms—if not in word, then in works, deeds and lives. Leaders can, and should, lead by example. In this manner I have heard great sermons preached and great prayers prayed when there was never uttered one word. (There are also* *many forms for conveying the words of Jesus: the press, television, radio and films.) Amen.*

The man Jesus in His day and time was called by theologians "a friend of sinners."

"The Son of man came eating and drinking, and they say, Behold a man gluttonous, and a winebibber, a friend of publicans and sinners. But wisdom is justified of her children" (Matthew 11:19).

These theologians were the deeply religious people of that day and time, the ones that supposedly held the religion in their hands, the ones that had a rational interpretation or a so-called perfect knowledge of God's relation to the world and to man. But they did not know or understand man's duty to God and man's duty to mankind. These "deeply religious" people concluded that Jesus was of no account or they had no use for Him.

Theologians, especially the half-baked ones that started the "God is dead" movement, are still a danger to the world — if their god is position, power, wealth and great fortune or if their goal is to worship themselves as a god, which is a puny and a poor god. I will spell that "god" with a small "g." One of the great dangers of the world today is to spell man with a capital "M" but to spell the true and living God with a small "g." The emphasis is in the wrong place.

When the lost souls stand before God during the judgment, however, the Bible says the small and the great that are lost will find out God is indeed alive.

"And then shall appear the sign of the Son of man in heaven; and then shall all the tribes of the earth *mourn*, and they shall see the Son of man coming in the clouds of heaven with power and great glory. And he shall send

his angels with a great sound of a trumpet, and they shall gather together his elect from the four winds, from one end of heaven to the other" (Matthew 24:30-31).

The world never heard a preacher like Jesus. He spoke with boldness and authority yet with such love and understanding. Jesus had, indeed, such love and understanding. He could look at men and see what was in them—their sin and evil, their successes and failures, their conflicts, their tensions and their weaknesses—but He did not pounce upon them because of their sins. With patience, love and understanding, Jesus would show them a new and better way of life.

Could this well be a good rule for parents, teachers and all of us? We should not be too quick to pounce on a child. With patience and love we should show the child a new and a better way of life—at least until tomorrow. Then, if no improvement is made, we should not spare the rod of discipline (in an acceptable form) to avoid spoiling the child.

What has made our great people be considered great? Great people have been more, but not less, than those who are all discreet and wise, partly by sheer ability and partly by being able to look about them, to see things that should be done and with boldness, faith, strength and courage in Christ to do them, regardless of the consequences. Most of all, great people have been those who are interested in humanity and the problems of the human race, in the fatherhood of God and the brotherhood of man.

When the kingdoms of this world are turned into the kingdom of Christ, then and only then will war be banished from the earth.

On the day Jesus was baptized by John, a voice from heaven, the voice of God, spoke.

"And Jesus, when he was baptized, went up straightway out of the water: and lo, the heavens were

opened unto him, and he saw the Spirit of God descending like a dove, and lighting upon him: And lo a voice from heaven, saying, This is my beloved Son, in whom I am well pleased" (Matthew 3:16-17).

Jesus has something very important to say to you. Did God mean for us to listen without believing, receiving and obeying?

CHAPTER 15

Read the Bible,
Pray and Minister to Others

If other preachers do not pray for our preachers, I thank God that our preachers pray for other preachers. If other churches do not pray for our church, I thank God if our church will pray for other churches. If other nations do not pray for our nation, I thank God if our nation will pray for other nations.

I wish I could stand on the walls of Zion and cry aloud to a world of lost and dying sinners with the words of John 3:16: **"For God so loved the world, He gave his only begotten son that whosoever believeth in Him should not perish but have everlasting life."**

Jesus said, **"Think not that I am come to destroy the law, or the prophets: I am not come to destroy, but to fulfill"** (Matthew 5:17).

Jesus said, **"For the Son of man is come to seek and to save that which was lost"** (Luke 19:10).

"When Jesus heard it, he saith unto them, They that are whole have no need of the physician, but they that

are sick; I came not to call the righteous, but sinners to repentance" (Mark 2:17).

Jesus said, **"The thief cometh not, but for to steal, and to kill, and to destroy: I am come that they might have life, and that they might have it more abundantly"** (John 10:10).

"Jesus said unto her, I am the resurrection, and the life: he that believeth in me, though he were dead, yet shall he live: And whosoever liveth and believeth in me shall never die. Believest thou this?" (John 11:25-26).

"Then spake Jesus again unto them, saying, I am the light of the world: he that followeth me shall not walk in darkness, but shall have the light of life" (John 8:12).

"And he saith unto them, Follow me, and I will make you fishers of men" (Matthew 4:19).

If mankind would obey Jesus, we would have done more for Him in twenty years than mankind has done in almost two thousand years. (Remember: This was written in the 1960s.)

> **Prayer:** *If we had followed You, dear Lord, we would not have any "-ism" or "-cism" in the world. Please help us to follow You more faithfully, more prayerfully. Amen.*

When families cannot get along, and members of a church cannot get along, then to ask the nations of the world to get along is a big order. Man cannot do this, but God could. No man can forgive sin or save. It is not my job to forgive; my job is the bringing. It is not my job to save; my job is the bringing of them to Christ where He can forgive and save. Save the lost and strengthen the saved with open minds and understanding hearts full of truth and full of grace.

Prayer: *I pray, O God, that individuals and nations will not pounce upon each other; but with patience, love and understanding they will show each other a new and a better way of life by not neglecting the poor and the needy, the old and the sick. Amen.*

I am not asking that society neglect the retarded, but I am asking them not to neglect the gifted. I do not ask for the law breakers to be denied their rights, but let us not forget that our blessed law-abiding citizens have rights also.

I love the wonderful song "God Bless America," and I love to sing it. But I also love to sing God bless the world, for God loves all people of all nations, and He is not willing that any should perish but all come to repentance. He is not slack, as most men call slackness, but long suffering to us. God will save us according to His promises, not our promises.

Jesus said, **"A new commandment I give unto you, That ye love one another; as I have loved you, that ye also love one another"** (John 13:34).

Prayer: *Give us love enough to forgive, even as Thou hast forgiven us. You know our desire. Purify our love, and let us behold the vision You have for us. Help us to be slow to anger and quick to understand, slow to criticize and quick to serve. Help us not to scorn the lowly or envy the great. Amen.*

Read the Bible and pray. It is good medicine for you, not only for the body, but it is also food for the soul. Try it and see how good it is for you and others. Read the Bible to people and pray with people in homes, hospitals, businesses, liquor stores, beer joints, honky-tonks or any place in which they will allow you to read the Bible and pray — and all the other places godly or ungodly. You name them; that is it. You try it. It will do more for you than I can tell you or probably you can imagine it will do for you for good. I will not try to tell you even a part of what you will come in contact with. It will not be all happiness or joy, nor will it all be disappointment and grief.

As for me I have not seen a single person ministering to others—no matter how heavy his grief or how difficult his burden to bear—to my memory, across my many long years of life, who has had a nervous breakdown or committed suicide. They have been so busy and concerned with others that they have not had time to think of themselves.

For example, I have worked all day in the office, and on my way home I would make two or three or perhaps a half dozen stops at sick homes or hospitals, some stops not over three minutes at a place, to read a few verses in the Bible and pray a short prayer, for a total of thirty or forty minutes in all. Then I would go home feeling as if I had not worked at all that day. I felt so good and rested. I felt as if I were walking on air.

You have got to do it to believe it. You have got to want to do it. Be honest and sincere in it with no misleading or deceit. When I left the office I was tired, but when I got home, after all those steps, I was not tired. I was rested and my soul blessed. No one can explain this. They just have to experience it. It is a good way to feel.

To know and believe—that is part of what the Bible means when it says this:

"For whosoever shall call upon the name of the Lord shall be saved. How then shall they call on him in whom they have not believed? And how shall they believe in him of whom they have not heard? And how shall they hear without a preacher? And how shall they preach, except they be sent? As it is written, How beautiful are the feet of them that preach the gospel of peace, and bring glad tidings of good things!" (Romans 10:13-15).

Prayer: *Save the lost and strengthen the saved. Amen.*

Open the Bible and read it. It has a message for you. Every word is true. Open the Bible and read it with an open mind and an understanding heart, for in it is not only truth about God but a way of life He would have all people everywhere to live.

Someone said, "The hand that rocks the cradle rules the world." I do not deny that. God bless our praying mothers, praying fathers and all people who pray. I pray there will be praying hands that rock the cradle so the world can be ruled in love, for then sin will be banished from the earth, and it will be filled with peace. Love is the answer.

* PART FIVE *

Life with Christ or Life without Christ

Prayer: *Help us, our Father, to be alert that we may avoid evil and love good. May we so commit ourselves that nothing will distract us from loving Thee. In Jesus' name we pray. Amen.*

CHAPTER 16

Doing All Things Well

His lord said unto him, "Well done, thou good and faithful servant: thou hast been faithful over a few things, I will make thee ruler over many things: enter thou into the joy of thy lord."
Matthew 25:21

We should be thankful for the good and beautiful things of life and for all those people who love them. I love the words of poet Edgar A. Guest: "Young men who are eager to rise in the world, listen to the tale I tell. Never put your hand to the least command unless you do it well. You must strive for speed, but speed is vain if poorly the work be done. The time you take for a good job's sake is time well spent, my son."

Prayer: *If it is Thy will, good Father, may the time hasten to come when one law shall bind all nations, and may that law be the universal law of brotherhood, the Fatherhood of God and the brotherhood of man, as taught by Thy beloved Son, in whom You were well pleased. For then and only then brotherhood will help to banish sin from the earth. Amen.*

God is love. Love is not God, but it is of God. God is life. Life is not God, but it is of God. God is light. Light is not God, but it is of God. God is the creator. The created are not God, but they are of God. So we should not worship the created; we should worship the Creator.

Little drops of water and little grains of sand make this big and mighty ocean and a whole world of land. I don't believe this will help those that do not need or do not want help, but I do believe it will help those that want help and need help.

When we are on our knees praying, let us pray as if everything depends on God; but when we stand on our feet to be counted, let us work as though everything depends on us. Let us pray prayers we can help God answer. Let us pray for good things. Let us ask God to give us health and strength to work as we go about doing good, until our mothers, sisters, daughters and wives will be safe and have a safe world in which they can live and make a living as we bring up our children in the way they should go. These are the children I have spoken of when I said, What can we blame them for? They are, as adolescents, held accountable for what they do, just as parents are today or grandparents were a generation or two in the past or a hundred or a thousand years in the past or will be for a hundred or a thousand years in the future.

Now then how good has the job of nurturing been done for you? How well will you do the job for the next generation? How pure, clean, honest, decent, good and willing to work will that generation be? The kingdom of God is more than this, but what would it be with what I have just mentioned? To me, life is one long school day. It is good to teach, but it is better to be teachable. I cannot help the big people; they do not need it. But I am trying to help the little people who need help.

It takes grains to make bushels, and it takes pennies to make dollars. Take care of the grains, and the bushels will take care of themselves. You can lead a horse to water, but you can't make him drink. You reap what you sew. If you want wheat, sow wheat. If you want corn, then plant corn. If you want potatoes, then plant potatoes. If you want clover hay, sow clover seed. If you want alfalfa hay, sow alfalfa seed. If you want soybeans, then plant soybeans. If you want to have sorghum molasses, then plant sorghum cane seed — and so on.

If you want to have something when you get old, save when you are young if you do not have a rich uncle. If you want health, obey the rules and laws for good health. It is better to stay well than to get sick and try to get well. No one, no matter how strong, can remain healthy by drinking whiskey, smoking cigarettes and doing many other harmful things too numerous to mention, but you know them. Live a healthy, long life.

As for me, I love to walk at least five miles a day. It is good medicine for me, and I was not born in this century. I never think of taking a sleeping pill. If five miles would not make me sleep soundly, then I would walk ten miles a day to sleep soundly. And another thing: my appetite is always uninvited. I do not have to take anything for an appetite, but I do have to watch my eating so that I do not eat too much. Working hard makes your food taste so good and makes you so hungry. I always loved to work hard and sweat. It always made me feel so good and healthy. After a good hot bath I feel so good and clean.

As we think, we are sure to become. Carefully cultivate your thoughts and your heart.

"Keep thy heart with all diligence; for out of it are the issues of life" (Proverbs 4:23).

I don't believe anyone ever went to heaven by himself; he took someone with him. I don't believe anyone ever went to hell by himself; he took someone with him.

Song: *When I leave this mortal shore, and mosey around the earth no more, don't weep, don't sigh, don't sob. I may have found a better job. Don't tell the folks I was a saint or any old thing that I ain't. If you have jam like that to spread, please pass it out before I'm dead. If you have roses, bless your soul. Just pin one in my buttonhole while I am alive and well today. Do not wait until I have gone away.*

CHAPTER 17

The Infinity of Influence,
Whether Good or Bad

S ome people seem to always stay a child, first childhood or second childhood, and never grow up. A smile is an inexpensive way to improve your looks. It is an old remedy.

Joke: *The prim old lady was given the first glass of beer she ever had. After sipping it for a moment, she looked up with a puzzled air. "How odd," she murmured. "It tastes just like the medicine my husband has been taking for the last twenty years."*

People do not go to heaven by themselves without taking others with them. People do not go to hell by themselves without taking others with them. What matters is not what man has done to us; it is what God has done for us. Through God's gracious power the orchards, fields, seas, forests and all the bounties of the earth are provided for our use. Let the grass of the fields and the flowers of the meadows be also our teachers. Let the earth before us and the sky over us be an open book we may read and so be wise.

If we think we are here for a long time, and enduring forever, some night let's look up at the little stars that have shined on millions of people in the human race that have so speedily passed on, and say within our own hearts this prayer: *We have only today or this moment. Help us to live it well as we try as best we can with Thy help to go about to do good, to help all Thy children everywhere to turn the kingdom of this world into the kingdom of Christ, a place where all people everywhere are safe, where they are interested in humanity and the problems of the human race. It will not be there then in heaven as it is here now.*

This is the attitude of many people: Just so my cup is full of sweet milk and cornbread, I do not care if your cup is full or empty. If my child is educated, I do not care if your child is educated or not. Just so I can make a living, I do not care if you make a living or not. If I can rear a wonderful family, I do not care if you rear a wonderful family or not. I know the good life, but do I want to keep it more than I want to share it with you? This is only a hint.

If individuals and nations run out of something good to do for themselves or their nations—with nothing more to be done in their sight for an individual or for a nation in the way of health, intelligence, character, cleanliness, purity, education, joy, peace, honesty, truth, mercy, light and love—then they should consider that there is an individual or a nation somewhere that is less fortunate than they are.

Help them to become interested in humanity and the problems of the human race so they will help those people and those children to have the things we have just mentioned. May their cup be also full. To me, this is one way of going about doing good deeds. That is what Christ did: He went about doing good works. There are battles to be fought and victories to be won, rather than waging war and killing people.

I thank God for my mother's prayers. If it had not been for Mother, where would I have been today? Only God knows. My mother believed in the Bible and prayer. She would say, "Do not kill. You can wipe the spit out of your face easier than you can wipe their blood from your soul." In daily living and testing times you can say just that when you are treated so very, very bad or even if they spit in your face. You can say in your mind, "If I could wipe your blood from my soul as easily as I could wipe your spit from my face, I might harm you."

I would so much rather see armies at home or away from home killing all the rats, mice, flies, mosquitoes, bean bugs, potato bugs and other things, such as germs, pests, blights to the fields, orchards, forest, land, air or sea. Increase the fertility of the soil, save and keep their soil, save their orchards and improve them, save their fields and crops of all kinds, and improve them and their harvest. This is a part of it. Also, it is a part of the abundant life Jesus was talking to us about. You could reach people's hearts this way. You cannot change people's hearts with bullets and bombs. How childish this is.

"And an highway shall be there, and a way, and it shall be called the way of holiness; the unclean shall not pass over it; but it shall be for those: the wayfaring men, though fools, shall not err therein" (Isaiah 35:8).

Jesus had such a depth of understanding that He could look at a man and see what was in him. He saw their conflicts, tensions and weaknesses. But He did not pounce upon them for their sins. With patience and love He would show them a new and better way of life. We cannot pray for the widow and orphan on Sunday and go out and rob them on Monday. God will bless those who love Him and keep His commandments.

If someone asks me how far my influence will go, I could not answer that. If someone asks me how long the wind will blow and how far a river would flow, I could not answer that either. A few years ago I was high in the Rocky Mountains looking down. In the distance was the silvery Colorado River, winding its way to the sea. The wind kissed my cheek and went on. I will say longer than the wind will blow and farther than the river will flow your influence will go on forever. Whether it is good or whether it is bad. Whether it is light or whether it is darkness. Whether it is love or whether it is hate. Whether it is life or whether it is death.

Prayer: *Save the lost and strengthen the saved. Amen.*

Please do not condemn me too much for not doing a better job on this writing, for if you only knew the conditions I am writing under you would understand and probably say, "How did he do anything at all?"

CHAPTER 18

Jesus: A Friend to Mankind

Do we want life without Christ more than we want life with Christ? Jesus can make people whole, the blind to see, the deaf to hear, the mute to speak and the lame to walk. He could heal the sick and raise the dead. Christ is our sufficiency. It is an individual affair, but the world will never be any better than the individuals who make it up. If all people everywhere should receive Him as their personal Savior, follow Him, walk with Him and please Him, then you would not recognize this old world.

Matthew 5:9 says, **"Blessed are the peacemakers: for they shall be called the children of God."**

If people turn the kingdom of this world into the kingdom of Christ, it will be the children of God who will do the job. I would like to help. Would you?

"What a friend we have in Jesus, all our sins and grief to bear. What a privilege to carry, everything to God in prayer" and "Through the storm, through the night, lead me on to the light. Take my hand, precious Lord, and lead me on" are a few lines from the many old church songs I heard my mother sing when I was a child. To this day they still mean so much to me.

> **Prayer:** *Blessed are they, O God, whose strength is in Thee. Help us to stand the strain of earthly cares; knowing in Thee is our strength, in daily living and in testing times. Help us to put our trust in Thee, the one who taught us to pray, "Our Father who art in Heaven." The trials, sufferings, hardships and sicknesses of life: may they lead us to Thee and not from Thee. Help us to profit by the written record of Thy Son's life and message. We ask this in the name of Thy beloved Son in whom You were well pleased, our master, teacher, redeemer, Lord and Savior. Amen.*

We know Christ as our teacher, but do we know Him as our Savior? May good conquer bad; may right conquer wrong. That is why we need a Savior within us. We need for Jesus Christ to be in us and for Jesus Christ to lead us. Christ will take out of us what should not be there, and He will not lead us where we should not go. This will keep the weeds out of our lives and help any life following Him to produce a good harvest. We must admit there are many dangers on the road of life. Life offers many different temptations and opportunities.

The Bible says, **"But now being made free from sin, and become servants to God, ye have your fruit unto holiness, and the end everlasting life. For the wages of sin is death; but the gift of God is eternal life through Jesus Christ our Lord"** (Romans 6:22-23).

That is why we need the Savior. There is something evil in everyone that will destroy them. But if we take Christ into our hearts and lives He will put out what should be put out and keep it out. On the other hand, Jesus will take into our lives what should be taken in and keep it there. Jesus will take us where we should go, and He will keep us from where we should not go. Jesus will help us do the things we should do, and He will keep us from doing the things we should not do. This does not leave anyone out. This means one and all.

"I Jesus have sent mine angel to testify unto you these things in the churches. I am the root and the offspring of David, and the bright and morning star. And the Spirit and the bride say, Come. And let him that heareth say, Come. And let him that is athirst come. And whosoever will, let him take the water of life freely" (Revelation 22:16-17).

Love is the answer for then and for now, for time and eternity. Jesus had a love: He could see in little children the kingdom of God. Jesus had a love: He could behold in a sinful woman a vision of purity. Jesus had a love: He could see in an uneducated fisherman a power that would shake the world. Jesus had a love: He could behold in a believing, repenting, dying thief—on a cross beside Him—an eternal soul. Jesus had a love: He could look with forgiving pity on those who crucified Him and ask God to forgive them.

"Then said Jesus, Father, forgive them; for they know not what they do. And they parted his raiment, and cast lots" (Luke 23:34).

Prayer: Jesus' love is a love I cannot understand, but I can receive it with thanks and say: *Give us love enough to forgive, even as You have forgiven us. You know our desires. Purify our love and let us behold the vision You have for us. Give us—all leaders and followers of all nations—a pure heart, a sound mind and clean hands. In Christ we pray. Amen.*

WHAT A FRIEND WE HAVE IN MOTHER

By P. M. Williams

What a friend we have in Mother,
Who will all our secrets share.
We should never keep things from her.
Tell her all, and she will be there.

Oh, what tender love she gives us
When in sorrow or despair.
Tell her gently, whisper softly.
She will listen; she will be there.

Day by day as she grows older
She's the nation's guiding star.
Don't forget the prayers she taught you.
You will need them where you are.

Though her hair has turned to silver
Send her flowers, sweet and fair.
Drop a card or send a letter.
She will be waiting; she will be there.

When her eyes have closed to slumber
Gently kiss her cold brow.
Fold her hands upon her bosom.
She will rest in heaven now.

When your days are dark and dreary
And your cross is hard to bear.
Do not let your memory fail you.
Think of Mother; she'll be there.

WHAT A FRIEND WE HAVE IN FATHER

By P. M. Williams

What a friend we have in Father
Who is always near and dear.
We should never disobey him
But love him with tender care.

Oh, he loves us just as Mother;
We should always love him, too.
Someday he will leave us forever.
Without him what would we do?

When his hair has turned to silver
Will you love him then as now?
Love him now while he is with you.
Death will someday cool his brow.

When he is old, we should respect him.
He deserves the very best.
Soon will come the day of judgment.
He'll be numbered with the blest.

When his eyes have closed forever
And you cannot view his face.
Mother, too, will then be older.
There's no one can take her place.

You will miss him at the table.
There will be a vacant chair.
If you love him, plainly show it.
For his days are numbered here.

PART SIX

FROM THE CRADLE TO THE GRAVE

Our Father who art in Heaven, help us to understand the cross and to accept the plan of salvation. Amen.

CHAPTER 19

God's Still, Small Voice

The unknown is greater than the known with all people everywhere. Jesus offered to us by the sacrifice of Himself upon the cross salvation for our sins.

"And Jesus answered them, saying, The hour is come, that the Son of man should be glorified" (John 12:23). Jesus also said, **"And I, if I be lifted up from the earth, will draw all men unto me"** (John 12:32).

> **Prayer:** *Our Father who art in heaven, help us to understand the cross and accept the plan of salvation. Amen.*

To the lost it is foolishness. To the saved it is the power of God unto salvation for all that will believe it, receive it and live it. When people believe Christ is the Son of God and accept Him as their personal Savior, that produces the spiritual birth. That is being born again. From that moment the saved person begins to live forever.

Jesus said, **"Fear none of those things which thou shall suffer: behold, the devil shall cast some of you into prison, that ye may be tried; and ye shall have tribula-**

tion ten days: be thou faithful unto death, and I will give thee a crown of life" (Revelation 2:10).

Consider this: *What was above the cross of Jesus, beneath the cross, to the right of the cross, to the left of the cross, in front of the cross and to the back of the cross?*

Above the cross of Jesus, we are endued with power from on high.

Those who forsake him and tarry **beneath the cross** will have woe, woe, woe.

To the left of the cross was unbelief, final rejection of Christ and eternal damnation.

To the right of the cross was the believing, repenting, eternal soul.

"And Jesus said unto him, Verily I say unto thee, Today shalt thou be with me in paradise" (Luke 13:43).

In back of the cross was an eternal rebuke to the designs of the ungodly.

And **in front of the cross** — for then, for now and for time and eternity — was the living Christ, our living Lord. Jesus proved conclusively to the world that there is life beyond the grave. We are not serving a dead God; we are serving a living God now and forever.

"Thy kingdom come. Thy will be done in earth, as it is in heaven" (Matthew 6:10).

What is the kingdom of God? It is more, much more, but it is not less, than when people have learned how to live together, with sound minds, clean hands and pure hearts.

Do we want to know more about outer space than we want to know about inner space? Do we want to know more about Jesus than we want to become like Him? I would love to live in God's kingdom on this earth with all nations and all people where we would be safe with no jails and no penitentiaries. The money wasted on sin could be used, instead, for a blessing to mankind and to God. Talk about the high cost of living. A sinful life is the costliest life ever lived. Sin causes wasted lives. It is not only the cost, but it is also the loss that is tragic.

Weep for the lost and pray: *O God, save the lost and strengthen the saved. Amen.*

I want to help turn the kingdom of this world into the kingdom of Christ. Do you? Will you follow Christ? He will help you to help the peacemakers around the world, to make this old world safe for all people everywhere to live in, a better world in which to live. The way of Christ is life, but the way of sin is death.

Oh, how I thank God for places where boys and girls, men and women, are safe. Just think: If we might have peace-loving people and tranquil places—where our mothers, our sisters, our wives and our daughters are safe and free from all harm—that makes my heart rejoice. That would be an improvement over what we have now. That would be a part of the abundant life Jesus was talking about.

But it takes work to produce a harvest like that. It also takes such work to produce a harvest of corn, wheat or hay. Weeds will grow with neglect. To grow the fruitful things requires attention, care, work and sweat. It is no harm to sit in the shade; but if you sit in the shade all the time, where will you be?

I will try to do my part. Work will win, and faith will work wonders. That is one reason I am trying so hard now to help people to be their best and give some of the best that is in them. Look for what is good in others. This is part of the process of producing a good life and a good harvest, for weeds grow in both.

I have had an awful time with myself to keep the weeds out of my life, for the devil is going up and down the earth like a roaring lion, seeking whom he may devour, with things that are pleasing to the eye, soothing to the ears. Smells good. Tastes good. Yes, it may even feel good and be very attractive, but beware. May God forbid, and He will through that still, small voice in a good, pure, clear conscience that is clean as pure snow. God places a conscience in the soul of every individual who has ever been born or ever will be born, if it has not been destroyed by the devil.

These are the words of the good and great teacher, Jesus, as found in the Gospel of John 8:44: **"Ye are of your father the devil, and the lusts of your father ye will do. He was a murderer from the beginning, and abode not in the truth, because there is no truth in him. When he speaketh a lie, he speaketh of his own: for he is a liar, and the father of it."**

We plainly see that God is the father of truth, but the devil is the father of a liar. Read the entire eighth chapter. It would bless your life if you would read the whole book of John. It has only twenty-one chapters in the entire book. With only thirty minutes of reading a day, two or three times in a week, you could read it through.

Read the New Testament through as often as you can. Each time you reread it you will get many new blessings with a new and better understanding of God's Word. Read the whole Bible through. That is a bigger and harder job. Your effort will pay.

It will bless you, and your life will be made richer.

CHAPTER 20

Attaining Success in Life

R ead the Bible and pray thoughtfully, mindfully and prayerfully. The Bible is not only truth about God and things eternal, but a way of life God would have us to live. I like to think we are either saved or lost, either going to heaven or going to hell. The difference is this: Whom do you love and serve? If you love God, you will serve Him. If you love the devil, then you will serve him. Choose this day whom you will serve. To serve God is life, but to serve the devil is death.

In John 8:42-43, Jesus said unto them, **"If God were your father, ye would love me: for I proceeded forth and came from God; neither came I of myself, but he sent me. Why do ye not understand my speech? even because ye cannot hear my word."**

In John 8:46-47, Jesus said, **"Which of you convinceth me of sin? And if I say the truth, why do ye not believe me? He that is of God heareth God's words: ye therefore hear them not, because ye are not of God."**

One of the consuming sins of the world today is the desire to get something for nothing or to eat without work or to provide all things in the sight of all men.

Everywhere I turn, there is the old deceiving devil to tempt me on every hand. Sometime for me to say the little word "no" is hard indeed. If I had lived all the bad thoughts that have gone through my mind, I no doubt would have been the meanest devil that ever lived. On the other hand, if I had lived all the good thoughts that ever went through my mind, I probably would have been the greatest saint that ever walked this earth.

Life without Christ is dangerous at any age. During the teen years many fathers and mothers do not understand their teenage children. Their teachers do not understand them. Their Sunday school teachers do not understand them. Their preachers do not understand them. Their doctors do not understand them. And last, but by no means least, they do not understand themselves. We know full well that it is not only the women and men and the old people who need Christ. It is also the youth, the children and the teenagers.

To leave the world in a little better shape than we found it: if I with God's help can lead one boy or girl, one man or one woman, to Christ, I feel I will be well paid for what I am trying to do. I hope and pray I leave this old world in a little better shape than I found it and that I bring out some of the best that is in every one of us. God loves us, needs us and wants us on His side and in His work among men, here and now. All people everywhere, laboring together in one bundle of love, will not be able to do a better job than God wants us to do for Him. God needs us here and now, right where you are, here on earth, while you are alive and well today. Please do not wait until you are sick, old or ready to go away.

Song: *When I leave this mortal shore, and mosey around the earth no more, don't weep, don't sigh, don't sob. I may have found a better job. Don't tell the folks I was a saint or any old thing that I ain't. If you have jam like that to spread, please pass it out before I am dead. If you have roses, bless*

*your soul. Just pin one in my buttonhole while I am alive and
well today. Please do not wait until I have gone away.*

Prayer: *We thank Thee, our Father and our God,
for all Thy people anywhere in this old world who
are walking with Thee and pleasing Thee. Shield and
defend them from the evil intentions of their enemies,
only as Thou knowest how. In Jesus' name, amen.*

Prayer: *Our Father, we thank Thee that Jesus
lives in our hearts. Help us to walk by faith and not
by sight. May we experience the reality of Thy love.
In Jesus' name, amen.*

The spoiler is among the works of the Almighty. I wish
and pray that I could in some way make it a little easier for
people to do what is right and a little harder to do what is
wrong.

Prayer: *Teach us, O God, how to become richer
among the beautiful things of life until we have
wealth untold to share with others. In Christ we
pray. Amen.*

Yes, we have attained success in life, those who have
learned to live well, love much and laugh often, those who
have learned to live in a way so they give some of the best
that is in them and look for something good in others. Yes,
they have attained success in life, those who have learned
to live in a way so they will leave the world a little better
than how they found it, regardless of whether it is a pleasant
smile, a good deed, a kind word. Perhaps they saved the
soil, increased the fertility of the soil, saved the forest and
improved a plant, a better grain, a finer fruit or a rescued
soul. On and on you name them, and that is it, such as a
perfect poem.

Prayer: *Dear Lord, help your workers and missionaries to cause the bad to be good, the ugly to be beautiful, the sick to be well, the liar to be truthful, the thief to be honest, the dirty to be clean, the filthy to be pure, and the lazy to work. In Christ we pray. Amen.*

CHAPTER 21

Wait Until I Get Ready Or Deathbed Repentance

Joke: Two little birds were sitting on a telephone wire, and one said to the other: Isn't it funny how some people's voices tickle your feet?

I will try as best as I can to stay away from all issues, Bible and otherwise, that require a doctor. The unknown is far greater to me than the known, but one thing I do know: I am sure it is good medicine to let all of us want to be on God's side, instead of wanting God to be on our side. In other words, let us not plan and plan, asking God to bless our plans and our ways, but see ourselves as we are. Ask God to help us get self out of the way, saying within our hearts: Not my will but Thy will be done, O God. For then and only then can God make us a blessing to His plan and His way. God is not willing that any should perish but all come to repentance.

Some people are great believers in this: When I get ready I will serve Christ. Others plan for deathbed repentance. I will not say that is impossible, but to me it is a very risky thing indeed. Look for a moment at that risky logic. Look at what those people do to themselves, to their God and to their fellow man. Can those wayward people not see what a loss they have been to themselves, to their God and to their fellow man? This "wait until I get ready" or "deathbed repentance" reminds me of someone who wants something of God for nothing.

The Bible says, **"Remember now thy Creator in the days of thy youth, while the evil days come not, nor the years draw nigh, when thou shalt say, I have no pleasure in them"** (Ecclesiastes 12:1).

Jesus said, **"Whosoever therefore shall confess me before men, him will I confess also before my Father which is in heaven"** (Matthew 10:32).

Jesus said**, "Be thou faithful unto death, and I will give thee a crown of life"** (Revelation 2:10). He did not say: I will give you a diadem crown. Jesus said, **"I will give thee a crown of life."** He said what he meant and meant what he said.

I want to call your attention to one of my many experiences in life, just a little peep through a crack in the curtain as I pull it back enough for you to get a glimpse of life, the ways of living. A man had position, power, wealth and great fortune. He was a big businessman, a banker and a lawyer, and as the world measures greatness he was at the top. It looked to me that he had health, intelligence and wealth beyond measure. This man told me he was not ready to take Christ into his life at that time, for he felt he could accumulate wealth faster without Christ than he could with Him.

"But when I make one more million," he said, "I will take Christ as my personal Savior."

He was of good intentions, I believe, but you will notice the two big "I's" he used: "when I" and "I will." I told him I felt the Spirit of God had led me to read a few short verses in the Bible to him and to pray. I asked if I could do that.

The man said, "Yes, but make it short, for I want to be in a stockholders' meeting in thirty minutes."

As I opened the Bible to Matthew 5:1-9, I said to him, "These are not my words. They are the words of the good and great teacher Jesus, and He speaks to us today from the written pages of the Holy Bible, just as much as He did when He walked the shores of the Sea of Galilee."

As I finished the ninth verse I said, "Here endeth the reading and hearing of His Word," and I closed the meeting, the personal contact, with these words: *"Our Father and our God, give us faith to believe and receive the truth that is in Thy Word with open minds and understanding hearts, for in it is not only truth about God and things eternal, but a way of life God would have us to live. In Christ we pray, amen."*

This man did not see the light of another day. That night he passed away.

Read those verses mentioned above in Matthew 5:1-9: **"And seeing the multitudes, he went up into a mountain: and when he was set, his disciples came unto him: And he opened his mouth, and taught them, saying, Blessed are the poor in spirit: for theirs is the kingdom of heaven. Blessed are they that mourn: for they shall be comforted. Blessed are the meek: for they shall inherit the earth. Blessed are they which do hunger and thirst after righteousness: for they shall be filled. Blessed are the merciful: for they shall obtain mercy. Blessed are the pure in heart: for they shall see God. Blessed are the peacemakers: for they shall be called the children of God."**

The Sea of Galilee receives and gives. It is alive. The Dead Sea receives and retains all; it is dead. Which one are our lives going to be like: the receiving and giving Sea of Galilee or the receiving and retaining Dead Sea? With Christ we will live. With Christ the whole world will live. It is an individual affair. Without Christ we will die. How do I know?

Jesus said, **"But go ye and learn what that meaneth. I will have mercy, and not sacrifice: for I am not come to call the righteous, but sinners to repentance"** (Matthew 9:13).

Jesus said, **"For the Son of man is come to seek and to save that which was lost"** (Luke 19:10).

Prayer: *Dear Father, help us to grow in faith and trust that we may live together in peace and hope. Help us to grow in love that we may share Thy life and message with others in victory through our Lord and Savior Jesus Christ. In His blessed name we do pray. Amen.*

PART SEVEN

THE GREAT SLOGAN

The pure in heart that pray together around the world
shall stay together forever in that world without end.

Sarah Catherine Williams
with doll and a duck on a leash.

CHAPTER 22

Life: One Long School Day

The fields of grain, the fields of clover, the meadows of grass, the orchards of fruit of all kinds, the work, care and harvest—one hundred years ago was so different then, more or less. Childhood was happy and free. Laugh and play while gathering flowers for Mother's bouquet—playing in the woods, fields and meadows so happy and free.

Think of the swing in the big apple tree with all those large red, good-tasting apples that tree bore, not only bushels but over the years many bushel-pounds of apples. Swinging, swinging, swinging beneath the old apple tree. That was childhood then, so happy and free.

When the wind blew down the old apple tree I did not laugh; I cried. And Mother—she did sigh when the wind blew down the old apple tree. Life holds tears as well as joy.

When I was a boy, the water got low in the pasture where my calf I thought so much of was grazing. He was used to drinking from the overflow, but the water got low. He tried to reach the low water and fell in and drowned, and I cried again.

I have cried over things I could not help, and I have cried over things I could have helped.

I had a dog I thought a lot of and loved. One day, as he was keeping watch at the house as he often did, Dad came home. There lay some dead fryer chickens, and my dog was next to them. Father was sure the good dog killed the chickens, so he stepped in the house, got the gun and killed my dog. Then he looked behind the chicken coop and saw what had killed the chickens: a dead weasel my dog had killed. Dad was so sorry he killed the good, faithful watchdog. I did not cry by myself on that occasion.

As a child with a broken heart, that taught me a lesson I remember to this day: Get understanding and try to be sure you are right. In other words, look twice before you jump. I could go on and on in my recollections of daily living and in testing times, but this is a glance in that direction.

Life is one long school day from the cradle to the grave, but the saddest of all is an individual, a home, a nation, yea, even the world, not following Christ, not trying to do His will. Walk with Him and please Him.

Jesus said, **"Come, take up the cross, and follow me"** (Mark 10:21).

The Bible states that Jesus looked at Jerusalem and wept as He repeated these words: **"O Jerusalem, Jerusalem, which killest the prophets, and stonest them that are sent unto thee; how often would I have gathered thy children together, as a hen doth gather her brood under her wings, and ye would not"** (Luke 13:34).

If they would have known how Jesus loved them and how they broke the Savior's heart, to think what they had been and what they were, to think what they had done and what they were doing. I can't find words to tell you what is in my heart.

Through these tear-dimmed eyes will you let me put my loving arms around you to protect you from all harm, as I whisper love and mercy, light and truth, devotion and faith, hope and trust, righteousness and salvation in your ears? This is how it pleases me for all people everywhere to live together. This is the abundant life. This is going about doing good. This is to seek and to save the lost. To the saved this is the power of God unto salvation. As they labor together in one bundle of love to turn the kingdom of this world into the kingdom of Christ, great will be the reward of the saved, as good fills the earth, as water fills the sea. But to the unsaved it is foolishness, and great will their destruction be.

The good life will pay well, here and now. It is not easy to get, nor is it easy to keep and live, or I have not found it to be easy, by any means, for me. Everywhere I turn I contact evil. On the other hand, everywhere I turn I find God or His children. It is a mixed affair. It is an individual affair, but what a difference it makes in an individual: a consciousness of God and a reverence and a respect for God and the things that belong to God.

The unsaved are saying, "Give us life without God." The saved are saying, "Give us life with God." For man to separate himself from God is bad, but for God to separate himself from man is much worse.

Jesus said, **"And whosoever shall exalt himself shall be abased; and he that shall humble himself shall be exalted"** (Matthew 23:12).

"Righteousness exalteth a nation: but sin is a reproach to any people" (Proverbs 14:34). The nation that forgets God shall perish, and the wicked shall be turned into hell. The Bible, to me, is saying to the world, "Repent for the kingdom of Christ is at hand."

Prayer: *Our Father, lead all the people of all nations to accept Christ as their Savior—Russia, China, America and all the others.*

That is a big order without Christ, but with Christ it is possible. No common tongue, no common traditional friendship, no common market, no common interest in humanity and the problems of the human race, but love will fill them all with faith, hope and trust. God can do it, but man must let God do the work through man, with God's Spirit.

Jesus said, **"Howbeit when he, the Spirit of truth, is come, he will guide you into all truth: for he shall not speak of himself; but whatsoever he shall hear, that shall he speak: and he will show you things to come"** (John 16:13).

When the Spirit of God comes into the hearts of mankind, then out go suspicion, doubt, dread and fear. These have been an ancient curse and a present shame to humanity and the problems of the human race around the world for then, for now, for time and eternity—with man and man's will, without God and God's will. God is not slack as most men call slackness.

CHAPTER 23

A Good Harvest and a Good Life

A good harvest and a good life: both require a lot of hard work and attention. There are a lot of weeds to be kept out of both. The harvest of the fields can be compared to the life of an individual. There are harmful things to both the cornfields and to the lives of people. Weeds are the harmful or destructive things that will grow with neglect to the fields, with no attention at all. But the good and the best take the best that is in us. That is what the love of God does for an individual, a home, a church, a nation and the world.

Not a single one mentioned will ever be any better than the individuals that make them up and the amount of Christ or the Spirit of God. Each individual should have a pure heart with a sound mind and clean hands. You and I will have to be developed into more than a hothouse plant that will be wilted with the hot sun or broken with the wind. To live the good life requires the best, the strongest—real girls and boys, real women and men—with the love of God within.

A sterling character is good soil in which a beautiful soul can grow, not into a hothouse plant, but a giant oak, large and powerful, tough and strong, that will be able to withstand the storms that are sure to break in later life. The winds of disappointment, the storms of passion, yea, even the hurricanes of disaster.

The good life is more, but it is not less, than conflict with evil. By living the good life, we will be conquerors. Every human indecency, human lawlessness, suspicion, doubt, dread and fear, poverty, ignorance, disease, crime, tyranny, communism, war, sin and evil: these are not only an ancient disgrace but a present shame to humanity and the problems of the human race. I think this is what an earlier warrior meant, and may his words be ours this day if man wants to turn the kingdom of this world into the kingdom of Christ. As I see it, this is the way to do God's will through righteousness.

The Bible says to me that righteousness takes an individual to heaven and not to hell. Sin takes individuals to hell. "Righteousness exalteth a nation, but sin is a reproach to any people" (Proverbs 14:34). The nation that forgets God will perish, and the wicked will be turned into hell. But righteousness, according to many people, has become too old-fashioned to use or too dirty to say. Could that attitude be the work of the devil? He is on the job; don't forget that.

The devil conducts his work in many ways. Among the main things is to discourage, dishearten and fill us with doubt if he can as he goes about, slurring God to man and slurring man to God and to one another, and he is an artist at that. It is another one of the jobs the devil can do exceptionally well. This is also an ancient curse and a present shame, to humanity and the problems of the human race.

If we are to escape the abyss, the deep, dark chasm, that those ancient old nations plunged into—Greece, Rome, Assyria, Babylon, Egypt and all the others—it will be because of all those who are working together in one bundle of love for the good life. Jesus went about doing good. I am thankful man is not the savior of the world. If he were, I believe he would pick evil over good.

Jesus said, **"But whosoever drinketh of the water that I shall give him shall never thirst; but the water that I shall give him shall be in him a well of water springing up into everlasting life"** (John 4:14).

Jesus said, **"All that the Father giveth me shall come to me; and him that cometh to me I will in no wise cast out"** (John 6:37).

"Behold, I stand at the door, and knock; if any man hear my voice, and open the door, I will come in to him, and will sup with him, and he with me" (Revelation 3:20).

"And I say unto you, Ask, and it shall be given you; seek, and ye shall find; knock, and it shall be opened unto you" (Luke 11:9).

I will not promise you the good life will be an easy life, for I have found it to be everything but easy. **"And he said to them all, If any man will come after me, let him deny himself, and take up his cross daily, and follow me"** (Luke 9:23). He did not say, "Follow Me, and we will have a picnic." If you live a godly life, you will suffer persecution.

It seems to me that man has to change. Man should do something for God, or God is going to do something to godless man. It is not what man has done to us, but it is what God has done for us. The spoiler is among the works of the Almighty. All the sin and evil in the world are an eternal rebuke to the designs of the ungodly. I wonder if the kingdoms of this world will still be standing a thousand years from now.

The works of the spoiler are not only an ancient curse but a present shame. But the works and the workers of the good life are not only an ancient salvation but a present blessing to humanity and to the problems of the human race. The saved are not only the salt of the earth, but the light and the hope of the world. This is only a part of it, but it gives you a glimpse of the good life or going about doing good works. Jesus' great teachings, principles and ideals are like a light shining on a distant hill. We may never reach them, but they will show us the way.

It is not what we are that is important; it is that which we hope to become.

Prayer: *Bless Thy people everywhere that love Thee and serve Thee and all that love one another and are laboring together in one bundle of love to turn the hearts of man to the heart of God, a saved people, full of health, intelligence, character and a willingness to work, with a sound mind, clean hands and a pure heart. In Christ we pray. Amen.*

CHAPTER 24

Sojourners in This Life

We are sojourners in this life, here for a short time, even if we live to be old. But we see and hear many things. That is only a part of it. Many things we do not see or hear, and many are not noticeable at all. Could the things we do not see or hear be greater than what we do see and hear? Do we believe the unknown is greater than the known?

I am not the tadpole trying to be the frog. I am not the tail trying to wag the dog. I am not trying to mettle, touch, harm or destroy. I am not trying to take anyone's position, power, wealth or great fortune from them and give it to someone else. But I am only thinking.

What are we without Christ? Are we small or great? The Word of God became flesh and dwelt among us. We will not be judged by our preachers, our denominations, our fine homes, our fine cars, by the amount of land we own, by the largest bank account, our position, power, wealth and great fortune or by more degrees to our names than anyone else.

"And I saw the dead, small and great, stand before God; and the books were opened: and another book was opened, which is the book of life: and the dead were

judged out of those things which were written in the books, according to their works" (Revelation 20:12).

"Blessed are the pure in heart, for they shall see God" (Matthew 5:8) and **"Blessed are the peacemakers: for they shall be called the children of God"** (Matthew 5:9).

It is a small thing and not very noticeable to watch people, old or young, children or grownups, to wash their hands and face. Some will do a good job and be clean, and this habit of cleanliness will make a difference in their looks and in their lives if you want to look into the future. I will leave it with you to answer what happens to the others that do not even half wash or get their hands and faces clean. Answer it for yourself. What I want to say is this: If you are interested in helping girls and boys, give them this little simple test, and perhaps it would not be noticed by the children. Would they even know they were taking a test or that an examination was being taken to them or many others? But you watch the ones who roll up their sleeves and roll down their shirt collars, wash not only their hands clean but their arms to their elbows. There are also some that not only wash their faces clean, their ears clean and behind their ears, but they also wash their necks clean as well. Cleanliness is next to godliness.

Now they may be from a log cabin. They may not know what it is to have a full cup of sweet milk and cornbread. They have only known a half cup of sweet milk and cornbread. If they would have had a full cup, it probably would have been shared with other children in the family. It could have been a large family, and all they have known in life was to share with others. Now if all the children in a family washed clean—what a blessing. But I have not found it that way, I am sorry to say. I am not asking you to neglect the ones that half-wash their faces, but I am asking you not to neglect the ones that were so clean, for they are your greatest men and women.

They are born right. They are already made. You do not have to make them. They are your leaders for a better tomorrow, for a better world in which to live. They are the best course.

We have all kinds of people. Someone said it takes all kinds to make up the world. I will not say it takes all kinds, but I will say all kinds are here. But I hope not to stay or not to stay long enough to see when they all separate themselves from God. That has been an ancient curse and a present shame to humanity and the problems of the human race. The spoiler is among the works of the Almighty, the works of God. What a waste in human life.

But in the cornfield I observed a few of many things. Corn planted too close to a tree with shade or corn planted in too shallow or poor a soil will not produce an ear of corn at all. Some of it did not make corn ears, no, not even good fodder. Some did not get high enough, when it tasseled out, for the bumblebee to whiz around the tassel without wearing their stingers out against the ground. They are wasted in a cornfield, especially stunted growth, storms, wind, beasts, varmints, gates left open, fences torn down, rogues, roguish stock, to tear fences down, that will come in and destroy your corn.

Anecdote: *A neighbor's old steer kept jumping in our cornfield. I got tired of it and shot him with beans. It broke his tail close to the but- end as he was filling himself on our green corn. That fall he was sold with a bobtail, and they tried to bring him through our farm; but they could not get him through with four men trying to head him. He would switch that stub of a tail, bawl and head for the other way. And that steer would run over you if you did not get out of his* *way. His name was Bawl before he was shot with beans, but after that they called him Stubby. His tail came off.*

There are a lot of wasted human lives. A wasted life: how pitiful. What a shame.

Prayer: *O God, save the lost and strengthen the saved. In Christ we do pray. Amen.*

* PART EIGHT *

Save the Lost and Strengthen the Saved

I've never understood why children are afraid of the dark
and men are afraid of the light.

CHAPTER 25

Life Out of Death

The Bible and history give us the names of world powers, the number of them and the names of their kings or rulers. If the last great world power is in existence today, I do not know its name. I do not know its ruler's name. I do not know if the ruler of the last great world is even born at this time. If he is, I do not know if he is a little child around his mother's knees.

The Bible says to me: **"And they shall fall by the edge of the sword, and shall be led away captive into all nations: and Jerusalem shall be trodden down of the Gentiles, until the times of the Gentiles be fulfilled"** (Luke 21:24).

You and I do not know—but God knows—what is in store and to take place between 190 and 2015 A.D. Does that mean God will take out of the hands of the Gentiles the task of converting this old world to Christ and put the job of turning the kingdom of this world into the kingdom of Christ into the hands of converted or Christian Jews?

I understand the Bible to say to me: What we as Gentiles have done at that job will be child's play or kindergarten work compared to what the converted or Christian Jews will do.

What nationality will this last great world power ruler be? I will not say, for I might just think I know. I have heard good and smart men say all Israel—the nation of Israel—will be saved. But to me the Bible means all men or all people that contend for and are counted with God will be saved. The Bible suggests that Israel will crush, but I do not understand that as I have heard it interpreted or explained.

To me, it means God or Christ and His people or His followers will be victorious. This is how and why Jesus could teach lessons, preach sermons and pray prayers. That would bring light out of darkness, bring order out of confusion, separate truth from falsehood, bring health out of sickness, bring strength out of weakness, bring faith out of foolishness or out of doubt. He could unite man with God in order to bring life out of death.

Jesus loved the disciples unto the end. Jesus knew Judas would betray Him, Peter would deny Him, and Thomas would doubt Him. Jesus knew they would forsake Him, but He loved them unto the end. Paul found Him faithful at all times and in all circumstances. I, too, have found this to be true. Jesus is faithful toward mankind.

Perchance you have met Jesus and have entered into His friendship. If so, you know what I have told you is true. If not, I would like for you to meet Him, this Jesus. Will you accept Him as God's beloved Son in whom God was well pleased and as your personal Savior, leader and Lord? If you will, I know God will be pleased and glad you did.

For God loves us, and God cares about us. He wants and needs one and all, but all do not want to follow Jesus. It is a hard life to live—I have found—but it will be easy to die by, and I would not want to die without it. Your faith can make you whole. A godly sorrow in the heart of men and women for their sins brings salvation to all that believe. But the Bible suggests that the nations that forget God shall perish, and the wicked shall be turned into hell.

With love or without love can you see the difference, or does it make any difference to you? Love is a great servant: what you love, how you love and whom you love. Is it love, or is it lust, and do you know the difference? If you do not, if anyone would tell you the difference, would you believe it? God is love, but love is not God.

If we say there can be no life without love, let us all say all human life should receive God. Then we will have mothers who would at least love their little babies as much as a mother dog under the floor loves her pups. If we say there is no life without love, consider life without God in many cases where parents kill their little children. There will be many a little fingerprint against them on the Judgment Day.

What about the great number of children born out of wedlock? Many of them are born unwanted. As for that matter, what about the unwanted children born in wedlock? They could not help how they came into this world; but as young people and as adults they can help what they do, and they will be held accountable for their sins and no one else. Will they do to others what has been done to them?

It is not what we are; rather it is what we hope to become that is important. It is not what man has done to us, but it is what God has done for us. Let us not worry over what we cannot help, but be thankful for what God has done for us. Know the difference and do something about it by walking with Jesus and trying to please Him. Do justly, love mercy and walk humbly with God.

"For whosoever exalteth himself shall be abased: and he that humbleth himself shall be exalted" (Luke 14:11).

I have always loved birds. I have loved to watch them sit, walk, run, fly and build their nests. I have loved to look at the eggs in the nest, look at and watch the young birds in the nest, and watch the mother bird feed her young. At the old spout spring across the stream, in under the shelter of a large rock, a peewee bird built its nest on the side of the rock, with moss, mud and so forth, low down to the ground. She laid her eggs and hatched her young.

Some way or somehow the mother bird received a broken wing and could not fly. I wonder if some mean boy broke her wing with a rock. Across the stream were berries and food, so I put a pole across the small stream so the mother bird could walk across, get food for her young and feed the little birds.

I noticed two large black ants crossing the pole from each end, and they met out near the middle of the stream. Neither one would turn and go back to the end, so they began to fight. As a result, both of the ants fell into the water below.

CHAPTER 26

Jesus: An Understanding Savior

And Jesus said, Are ye also yet without understanding?
(Matthew 15:16)

If we are lonely, remember the Master knows for He was lonely. If we are forsaken, remember Jesus knows for He was forsaken. If we are falsely accused, remember Jesus knows for He was falsely accused. If we suffer, remember Jesus empathizes for He suffered.

Consider loneliness in an individual, in a church or in a school. I have had many experiences with loneliness in many places and in many ways.

If you would have friends, you have heard said, and so have I, first appear friendly yourself, but I have not always found this to be true. I have always been accused of being overly friendly. I have spoken to many people in church and out of church who did not speak to me. I have long since gotten out of the habit of having to pick up some good old sanctified person's hand, and if it was shook I would have to shake it myself. Someone who is so good and his face so long, I could not tell if it was a vinegar fruit, a sour pickle, a crab apple or a green persimmon. Did he want to whistle, or was he looking at me and got that expression or faraway look he had? Some people make you feel so cold. Someone told me they could skate down the aisle on ice, but I have not seen that myself.

The preacher told us one day that he visited some fine folks. I guess they were so much better out of the church than we were in the church. The preacher said he visited those newcomers to our town and could get them for new members to our church or to join our church if it were not for the kind of people that some of our members were. I wanted those newcomers to come and set us an example to go by or set us a mark to shoot at. I think some of the members did get them to join our church.

Eventually we lost our preacher because he left for an opportunity to earn more money. The pasture was greener over the fence or otherwise. But that old story went on. He might have stayed a little longer at our church, but just the same, if we had members more to his liking. I was never able to tell for sure—if we were better or worse off by getting the good people in the church, and if we bad ones made the good ones bad, or if we got the bad ones in the church, and the good ones made the bad ones good.

You will always find the best people in church, regardless of who says what. I have found it that way. Even if you are in the church, it will not make you immune from slander of the devil. One of his primary jobs is to slander God to man, to slander man to God and to slander man to one another. Slander causes trouble, even in some homes and in some churches and with some of the members in the same church, in some cases.

In some cases, the devil's tongue might slander some of the church's hardest fighters against the devil, especially if the devil sees and knows that church member is giving him a black eye and fighting him too hard. The devil can get the members in the same church to repeat this slander of his. He can work that way. He can almost deceive some of the very elect. If you ever fight sin and evil to that point, you will be very lucky. If you have more than your pastor and only one member of your church to come to your rescue and perhaps one church member from only one other church, it may be to the point where you may be having a terrible struggle with the devil.

The devil might be riding you with not only one spur but two spurs at the same time and not only spurring you with one spur at a time but with two spurs at the same time. It could be possible you would be praying for God to help you do what you should do and not what you wanted to do to the one the devil had used to lie about you and slander you so. The devil is the father of lies. The devil works through people who have never repented, but God only works through people who have repented.

A godly sorrow in the heart of man for sin works repentance unto salvation. That is what makes even bad people good people and nice people. It is indeed a great gift from God to man. What would we do without our friends, especially our Christian friends? You will never be lonely with even one friend you love and even one friend who loves you.

How I wish, hope, trust and pray that I could bring happiness to all people. How I wish I could bring all people to Christ where He could forgive them and save them. My job is the bringing, not the forgiving. My job is the bringing, not the saving. But if I can bring only one I feel I will be well paid for all the tears I have shed and all the prayers I have prayed, in writing this little message or a part of what is in my heart.

I have been told that a Christian can witness to the unsaved until your head drops off, and, in many cases, it will still do no good. But I can try, and if they go to hell then they cannot say truthfully that old Chum did not make it plain to them. I have been told, "If you would keep your mouth shut you would not let people know you were such a fool." But I can try.

Perhaps this talk goes with the trade of discouraging people. That could be the wedge the devil drives in people to split them apart. There is, as I have observed, a little bad in the best people and a little good in the worst of us. There is some ignorance in the intelligent and some intelligence in the ignorant. I am speaking for myself; I am not speaking for you or others.

I never in my life remember attending a graduating class in high school or college, when I was watching the seniors march, that this thought would run through my mind: If all the ignorance in that class were in one person, what would we have? And then, on the other hand, if we had all the intelligence in that class in one person, what would we have?

CHAPTER 27

Position, Power, Wealth and Great Fortune

What can bless a person's soul, an individual human being, more than reading the Bible and praying— thoughtfully, mindfully and prayerfully, with an open mind and an understanding heart—for in it is not only truth about God and the things eternal, but a way of life that God would have us live.

The life and message of Christ, not only in word, but in work, deed and life, from a pure heart, are indeed the answer to all questions and the solution to all problems, for here and now, for time and for eternity, for an individual, a family, a church, a nation, yea, for even the whole world. Whosoever will do the will of God and teach men or others to do the will of God will be the greatest in the kingdom of God or the kingdom of Christ, which is all the same.

"Whosoever therefore shall break one of these least commandments, and shall teach men so, he shall be called the least in the kingdom of heaven: but whosoever shall do and teach them, the same shall be called great in the kingdom of heaven" (Matthew 5:19).

This is a great and daring faith, to keep the commands of God. To the lost it is foolishness, but to the saved it is the power of God unto salvation to all that believe. The saved alone cannot turn the kingdom of this world into the kingdom of Christ. The world also needs the lost to let Christ save them in order to be complete and full. The pitiful thing about all this is sin: man separating himself from God. That is an ancient curse and a present shame.

"Verily I say unto you, I have not found so great faith, no, not in Israel. And I say unto you, that many shall come from the east and west, and shall sit down with Abraham, and Isaac, and Jacob, in the kingdom of heaven. But the children of the kingdom shall be cast out into outer darkness: there shall be weeping and gnashing of teeth" (Matthew 8:10-12). When God separates Himself from man there will not only be wailing, weeping and gnashing of teeth; but they will be in hell, and God has the keys to hell.

"For the wages of sin is death; but the gift of God is eternal life through Jesus Christ our Lord" (Romans 6:23). There are only two choices, the Bible tells us: with Christ and heaven, or with the devil and hell. Which will your choice be this day? Choose you this day whom you will serve. No children of God will ever worry about the devil attempting to put them into hell, for God has the keys to hell.

"And if it seem evil unto you to serve the Lord, choose you this day whom ye will serve; whether the gods which your fathers served that were on the other side of the flood, or the gods of the Amorites, in whose land ye dwell: but as for me and my house, *we will serve the Lord"* (Joshua 24:15).

Position, power, wealth and great fortune with Christ is an abundant life, a blessed life, an educated life, a useful life, a saved life, a life that goes about doing good. That is what Jesus did. He went about doing good deeds. But human nature then was as now: sinful. The powers of the lost, the powers of the world, of sin, allied themselves against Christ, His disciples and His followers to keep them from turning the kingdom of this world into the kingdom of Christ.

If you want to know the rules for the kingdom of God on this earth, the laws for it, for here and now or for time and eternity, you will find them in the Sermon on the Mount, in Matthew 5–7. Read all three chapters if you want the heart of Jesus' life and message and not only Matthew 5:1-9.

Also let's look at position, power, wealth, great fortune and education without Christ. Where will we be, and what will we have? You do not have to be poor and uneducated to go to heaven. Now then neither do you have to be educated and rich to go to hell.

Jesus said, **"Blessed are the pure in heart: for they shall see God"** (Matthew 5:8).

All those who do justly, love mercy and walk humbly with God will be saved. At this time we do not have enough saved people to turn the kingdom of this world into the kingdom of Christ. It will take the saved we have now to lead the lost to Christ, or it will take all the saved to lead all the lost to Christ, where Christ can save the lost.

Prayer: So many times in my prayers people have heard me say, *"Save the lost and strengthen the saved. In Christ we pray. Amen."*

I am thankful for all that do not scorn the lowly or envy the great. Love and be thankful for all the pure in heart, for not only God loves them, wants them and needs them, but we also should be proud of them, love them, want them and be thankful for them. We do surely need them to help us make this world a better place in which to live and to help people to live.

We should help our own church and denomination, but we should also be interested in helping and loving all churches and denominations. Love our people and love all people. Love our nation and love all nations, not only a common market for a few but a common market for all people and all nations. They also need a cup of sweet milk and cornbread.

Joke: *A man with his wagon and team of horses was going along the road one day. He met a fellow and said, "How far is it to the top of this hill, Buddy?" And Buddy replied with a twinkle in his eye, "Hill and thunder-ation! Man, your hind wheels are off of your wagon!"*

Now then that reminds me very forcibly of an individual with Christ or an individual without Christ. An individual without Christ has his hind wheels off. But all is well with the individual with Christ. An individual with Christ goes about benefiting himself and benefiting all people everywhere. The world will never be any better than the saved people who are in it. Likewise, the world will never be any meaner than the lost people who are in it.

To be sick is bad, but to be always sick is worse. To be blind is bad, but to be always blind is worse. To be deaf is bad, but to be always deaf is worse. Not to have understanding is bad, too, but never to have understanding is worse. To be poor is bad, but to be always poor is worse. To be lazy is bad, but to be always lazy is worse. To sit in the shade is not bad, but to sit always in the shade would be worse. To play a game of ball or to play marbles is not bad for a pastime, but if we played our lives away, where would we come out if we were not paid for it? To be lost is bad, but to be always lost is worse.

* PART NINE *

A Sterling Character

Let us all have a sincere interest in all people everywhere. May God help us to be interested in humanity and the problems of the human race.

CHAPTER 28

The Abundant Life

The kingdom of God, Jesus said, is within you. It is an individual affair. You will not have to take a trip to a far-off country or to outer space. It is inner space. It is within you.

"And when he was demanded of the Pharisees, when the kingdom of God should come, he answered them and said, The kingdom of God cometh not with observation; neither shall they say, Lo here! Or, lo there! For, behold, the kingdom of God is within you" (Luke 17:21).

It is not what man does to you on the outside. It is what God does to you on the inside. It is not what man does to you; it is what God does for you. The kingdom of God is more, but it is not less, than an individual full of truth and full of grace going about doing good deeds: a person that will not harm you. This type of person does not pose a threat to our mothers, our sisters, our wives and our daughters. This type of person would not deceive, slander or harm himself, his God or his fellow man.

The kingdom of God is more than–much more than, but not less than–happiness, righteousness, joy, peace, love and service in the Holy Spirit that will lead us in the ways of all truth, faith and grace. It is a gift from God, a free gift. We do not pay money for it any more than we pay money to God, who sends the rain for our harvest in the fields. The rain is just as necessary for the harvest in the fields as the Spirit of God is to the growth and harvest of our souls. The fields are white with harvest, and the laborers are few.

Where would we be without rain for our harvest in the fields? And where would we be without the Spirit of God for our souls?

Important: *A sterling character is good soil in which a beautiful soul can grow.*

"As the rain cometh down, and the snow from heaven, and returneth not thither, but watereth the earth, and maketh it bring forth and bud, that it may give seed to the sower and bread to the eater, so shall my word be that goeth forth out of my mouth; it shall not return unto me void, but it shall accomplish that which I please, and it shall prosper in the thing whereto I sent it" (Isaiah 55:10-11).

Also read John 10:1-11 and Job 19:1-29. Here are some excerpts.

"I am the door: by me if any man enter in, he shall be saved, and shall go in and out, and find pasture. The thief cometh not, but for to steal, and to kill, and to destroy: I am come that they might have life, and that they might have it more abundantly. I am the good shepherd: the good shepherd giveth his life for the sheep" (John 10:9-11).

"For I know that my redeemer liveth, and that he shall stand at the latter day upon the earth: And though after my skin worms destroy this body, yet in my flesh

shall I see God; whom I shall see for myself, and mine eyes shall behold, and not another; though my reins be consumed within me" (Job 19:25-27).

Anecdote: *Humbly look to God. The crops were beautiful, but the cracks in the ground and the brown tips on the leaves gave evidence that unless there was a rain soon our crops would die. We had often talked of rain, heard the thunder, seen lightning at a distance, but the clouds would always pass over. Finally the air was fragrant, and we rushed to the door to see the rain pouring down. How refreshing it was! How thankful we were! What a blessing it was! How helpful it was! How it was needed! Nothing could take its place.*

We often speak about God, see indications of His near-ness and share many good thoughts in our daily conversa-tions; but without the outpouring of His Spirit our hearts are parched and our lives unfruitful. Nothing can take the place of the refreshing and fruit-producing Spirit of God. Without the outpouring of God's Spirit we could not have a fruitful harvest of lives. We should know God and thank Him for sending the Savior of mankind to this earth.

Jesus came to reveal His loving heart to us and His concern for us. We should welcome and be thankful for the Comforter within us. We should want to know more about Jesus and want to become more like Him through reading the Bible, sermons, song, prayer and meditation. Not only our words—but our works, deeds and lives—should speak of His love and mercy, His light and truth, His devotion and faith, His righteousness and salvation.

For God's sake let us leave this "religion" out of the picture as we think for a moment together. The life and message of Christ are marred with the word "religion." Jesus offers a way of life, an abundant life, full and running over.

The jails and the penitentiaries are full of religion, but empty of salvation. They are not full of truth and full of grace.

"I am come that they might have it (life) more abundantly" (John 10:10).

"For the Son of Man is come to save that which was lost" (Matthew 18:11).

"And Jesus answering said unto him, Suffer it to be so now: for thus it becometh us to fulfill all righteousness. Then he suffered him" (Matthew 3:15).

"But when Jesus heard that, he said unto them, They that be whole need not a physician, but they that are sick. But go ye and learn what that meaneth, I will have mercy, and not sacrifice: for I am not come to call the righteous, but sinners to repentance" (Matthew 9:12-13).

"For the Son of man is come to seek and to save that which was lost" (Luke 19:10).

"Jesus saith unto him, I am the way, the truth, and the life: no man cometh unto the Father, but by me" (John 14:6).

"Jesus said unto her, I am the resurrection, and the life: he that believeth in me, though he were dead, yet shall he live: And whosoever liveth and believeth in me shall never die. Believest thou this?" (John 11:25-26).

"Go ye into all the world, and preach the gospel to every creature. He that believeth and is baptized shall be saved; but he that believeth not shall be damned" (Mark 16:15-16).

Through the Scriptures we can see Jesus, hear the words Jesus spoke and gain understanding, wisdom and salvation. To leave this body of flesh, for a child of God, is only a change of address, and it is a beautiful change for every child of God.

"For the Lamb which is in the midst of the throne shall feed them, and shall lead them unto living fountains of waters: and God shall wipe away all tears from their

eyes" (Revelation 7:17). Jesus can take His blessed nail-scarred hands and wipe the tears from our eyes, so we can see more clearly the joy of His salvation.

"And God shall wipe away all tears from their eyes; and there shall be no more death, neither sorrow, nor crying, neither shall there be any more pain: for the former things are passed away" (Revelation 21:4).

The higher a man is in grace, the lower he will be in his own esteem. Changed lives bring about a changed individual, a changed home, a changed society, a changed nation, a changed world. If we are too proud to confess we are lost, how can we expect God's help? The Father's redeeming love seeks us out where we are. When we follow Jesus, we walk in the way of redeeming love. We are safe. We will not stumble, for He knows the way.

"Through the storm, through the night, lead us on to the light. Take our hands, precious Lord, and lead us on" (words from an old church hymn).

Have I allowed God's redeeming love to change my life? Christ loves and welcomes all sinners. Why do we hesitate to seek His redemption through repentance? A godly sorrow in the heart of man works repentance unto salvation. Without God's forgiving love we would have no hope of redemption. When we give ourselves to Christ, undeveloped talents blossom into use, and that will produce a fruitful harvest of souls of the beautiful things of life. The God-forgiven heart is a pure, clean heart, full of truth and full of love and grace.

Prayer: *O, God, give us pure hearts. Amen.*

CHAPTER 29

Jesus: The Greatest Physician

The daily harvest occurs amidst all the dangers and storms of life. The winds of disappointment will buffet us. The storms of passion will tempt us. Christians must labor together, in one bundle of love, to keep the stream of life pure. That is the only way.

God in His great wisdom provided for the human race to beautifully color the stream of human life that would flow down through the future time. That is indeed a wonderful work and accomplishment as to what God can accomplish through man. An individual with Christ makes a difference. Christianity changes things. Peacemakers want to remove stumbling blocks.

Anecdote: *I remember a fellow was trying to go about doing good deeds, and he worked to have voting in order to ban whiskey in his community. In the process the activist almost lost his life while working to get it done. He waged a vigorous campaign. He made a hard fight to get a dry vote. One day, at the close of a speech, a big whiskey dealer said to him, "That was the worst talk I ever heard a man make." But the speaker thought the whiskey dealer's comment was one of the best compliments he had ever received in life.*

When we fight sin hard enough we should expect the lost to be against us and not only criticize us but slander us as well. If they never repent and turn to God they will always be our enemies. When we preach sermons, teach lessons and pray prayers, if people, particularly lost people, tell us our words were the sweetest they ever heard, can we be sure we are doing God's will and doing our duty as a Christian? Do we think that would be our best compliment or our worst compliment?

Prayer: *Give us a fruitful harvest, O God. Amen.*

Many centuries before Christ, history tells us that alchemists, the Egyptian chemists, spent their lives trying to turn base metals into gold. Jesus was the greatest chemist the world has ever known. Jesus could turn the physical into the spiritual. Jesus could turn the perishable into the immortal. I could go on and on, but this is only a glimpse to get you to stop, look and listen. Just look in that direction. You can elaborate more on those thoughts.

Important: *Jesus was the greatest physician the world has ever known.*

I told that statement to a doctor one time, and he said, "If you want help, call on me or another doctor; don't call on God." But that did not change my mind one iota. I still think our good doctors and skilled surgeons—with their knowledge, skills and arts—are needed very much. But I still believe God, through nature, is the greatest healer and restorer to health. The patient, the doctor, God and time are all important. The doctor can come back to us and at us in many ways and say to us, "You should have seen the patient when God had him by himself," in the case of an inflamed appendix, blood poisoning and so forth.

But we could say that also about a field of corn before it was cleared, plowed, planted, cultivated, thinned, plowed and cleaned of the weeds. When the field is properly prepared and tended, we can see the results of work, cultivation and rain. God has done much for us. We could say, "What a field of corn God has given us, and we are thankful."

Anecdote: *We could, as my daddy told a preacher one day as he was bragging about what a field of corn God had given him. My father, his face and shirt and pants wet with honest sweat, tipped his old straw hat back from his fore-head and with the forefinger on his left hand passed it over his forehead, causing a great stream of honest sweat to fall to the ground. My father said these words: "Brother Pete, you should have seen this field before I cleaned it up, when God had it by Himself."*

Work will win, and faith will work wonders. Faith to the lost is foolishness, but to the saved it is the power of God unto salvation. To obey the commands of God is a great and daring faith. Jesus said, **"If ye love me, keep my commandments"** (John 14:15), and **"Ye are my friends, if ye do whatsoever I command you"** (John 15:14).

"Then said Jesus unto his disciples, If any man will come after me, let him deny himself, and take up his cross, and follow me" (Matthew 16:24). Do we want Jesus to follow us more than we want to follow Him?

To follow Jesus is not easy, but we can do all things through Christ who strengthens us. **"I can do all things through Christ which strengtheneth me"** (Philippians 4:13). You are not going on a picnic or a vacation. It will take toil, sweat, blood and tears. It will take tired arms, legs, backs and bodies. It will take many falsehoods told on you. You will be slandered much. You will be forsaken. You will suffer. You will be spit on. You may become discouraged.

But remember: *Jesus knows, for He suffered through all this and much more.*

In the morning, however, Jesus stood on the shore: *a morning, a Savior and a shore.* If we are on Jesus' side, all is well. But if we want Him on our side, look out! Ouch!

Prayer: *We thank Thee, O God, that Thou sent the Savior of mankind to this earth to reveal Thy loving heart to us and Thy concern for us. Help us to know Him better, through Thy Word and through sermons, songs, prayers and meditations. May not only our words but our works, deeds and lives speak of His love and mercy, His light and truth, His devotion and faith, His joy and peace, what is clean and pure, and His righteousness and salvation. In Christ we pray, amen.*

CHAPTER 30

God: Man's Best Friend

In order to make this old world God's, this is the type of
life it will take, and this is the leadership we must have:
all people with Christ, and none without Christ. Then and
only then will you see a good and great people interested in
humanity and the problems of the human race. Then where
will our problems have gone? Love will have swallowed
them up in victory.

Love is the answer. Let us replace love for hate. Many
more substitutions are greatly needed: good for bad, safety
for danger, truth for falsehood, honesty for dishonesty, pure
lives for impure lives. Transformations are needed: light
out of darkness, the clean from the unclean, order out of
confusion. May man one day be united with God: all men,
all nations, all people, kindred and tongues—united in one
bundle of love—with sound minds, clean hands and pure
hearts. May we have one common tongue of love, one
common heart of love, one common market, and hands of
prayer, praying hands that will help all and harm none.

Try to live Christian lives and help all to live Christian
lives. Try to make an honest living and try to help in some
way or somehow that all can make a living. Not only my
cup full of sweet milk and cornbread, but try in some way or

somehow that all people everywhere have their cups as well to be full of sweet milk and cornbread. This is for people like me and the teeming millions like me around the world who would be thankful for a full cup or even a half cup. This is not for the ones that would turn their nose up at this kind of eating. They eat higher on the hog, or they may be eating the fatted calf.

Things are changing. If we are following Christ, all is well, and the children of God are turning the kingdom of this world into the kingdom of Christ.

Jesus said, **"Blessed are the peacemakers; for they shall be called the children of God"** (Matthew 5:9).

Anecdote: *When I was a boy, Father would clean the old lantern, trim the wick, fill it with oil, clean the globe and light the lantern. It would give a bright light to walk by in the dark. We would start out in the darkness of the night for different things and on different missions—sometimes a coon hunting, sometimes to see the sick—and Father would say, "Now, boys, stay behind the light or behind the lantern, and you can see how to walk. You can see where you are stepping or where you are going so you will not stumble. But if you get in front of the light you will stumble, for you cannot see where you are going." So it is with Christ.*

Jesus said, **"Follow me."** If we will follow Him, we can see where we are going, for He knows the way; but if we get in front of Jesus, we will stumble.

God blesses praying hands, raised in reverent devotion. Consider a sound mind, clean hands and a pure heart. Consider a long, hard life of honest, hard work and toil. Compare a life with God and a life without God. Man is man's worst enemy, but God is man's best friend.

It is too terrible to call to mind regarding even a small part of what man without God has done to himself, to his fellow man and to his God. This has been an ancient curse and a present shame. God's people have lived through periods of history, hundreds of years ago, beset by problems. Then as now people had to make difficult adjustments to new ideas, discoveries and inventions and to sudden changes to social and economic life.

Early in the sixteenth century Martin Luther rose against errors and abuses. He openly condemned the Roman Church and gave impelling force to the Reformation movement. Millions of Christians gained a new spiritual freedom, but not without struggle and bloodshed for all those who took their stand and fought for the purity of the Word of God. When it appeared that Luther was taken prisoner and might die as a martyr, many prayers were prayed.

Our bitterly divided world is in need of prayer. As we draw near to God in sincere confession, He takes the burden of sin from our hearts and grants us courage. We do not pray for ourselves only, but for all who desperately yearn for peace in our troubled world. We know that the plight of the homeless, the hungry and the oppressed calls for hands willing to work, as well as for hands willing to pray. We show through deeds of brotherly love our gratitude for the gifts we have received—gifts of body, mind and worldly goods.

We need never feel alone. A fellowship of faith unites us with Christian men and women across land and sea upon the face of the whole earth. Meditating, working and praying with millions of others, we can safely put our trust in God who gave His only begotten Son for the redemption of all mankind and whosoever will receive Him as their Lord and Savior.

Today, as always, God holds the whole troubled world in His hands. This is God's world. He made it without man's help. God, as a great loving Father, has tried to build His kingdom here on earth, regardless of how man has tried to unmake it. Man reeled against it, and the lost allied with the world powers against God's will being done on earth as it is in heaven.

What is God's will? **"The Lord is not slack concerning his promise, as some men count slackness; but is longsuffering to usward, not willing that any should perish, but that all should come to repentance"** (2 Peter 3:9).

God filled His world with beauty, wonder and a little more goodness than some of us might imagine. **"And God saw every thing that he had made, and, behold, it was very good. And the evening and the morning were the sixth day"** (Genesis 1:31).

Prayer: *May we not ask Thee to do for us what we can do for ourselves. Amen.*

God knows more and better what we need than we know to ask Him ourselves.

Prayer: *Help us to step from the busy cares of life long enough to see Thy beauty, absorb some of Thy wonder and add a little to Thy goodness. Then we should be glad and in our hearts give thanks. Amen.*

CHAPTER 31

The Meaning of Jesus' Life

Let us not faint when trying, as best as we humanly can, to follow Christ and do what is right and best. **"And let us not be weary in well doing: for in due season we shall reap, if we faint not"** (Galatians 6:9).

"For God hath not appointed us to wrath, but to obtain salvation by our Lord Jesus Christ, who died for us, that, whether we wake or sleep, we should live together with Him" (1 Thessalonians 5:9-10).

Quotation from the sixteenth U.S. president: *Abraham Lincoln wisely stated, "Do what conscience says is right. Do what reason says is best. Do your duty and be blest."*

The Bible says, **"Let us hear the conclusion of the whole matter: Fear God, and keep his commandments; for this is the whole duty of man. For God shall bring every work into judgment, with every secret thing, whether it be good, or whether it be evil"** (Ecclesiastes 12:13-14).

Do not think you will be pleased and encouraged by all people, even by visiting awful people in terrible places. And it is possible the deeply religious people will have something to say about the good you have failed to do—if they know about you going into the home of a drunkard, reading the Bible and praying in that home, and if they see that man drunk or both of you at the same time. The person knows you have been going to that home, reading the Bible and praying. Do not let it discourage you or stop you if it is said to you, "Isn't that one of your converts?" You can only say, "It looks like one of mine. It certainly is not one of God's."

Life without God is an ancient curse and a present shame, but life with God is an ancient blessing and a present salvation. God is man's best friend. The devil is man's worst enemy. Choose this day whom you will serve.

"And if it seem evil unto you to serve the Lord, choose you this day whom ye will serve; whether the gods which your fathers served that were on the other side of the flood, or the gods of the Amorites, in whose land ye dwell; but as for me and my house, we will serve the Lord" (Joshua 24:15).

It is an individual affair. It is your choice whom you will serve and where you will spend eternity. If there were not a heaven or a hell at all, it would still be so much better to live a good life here and now. Man with God is man's and God's best friend. But man without God is man's and God's worst enemy.

Do not worry yourself to death about what man has done to you, but be thankful for what God has done for you—with love enough to forgive, even as God has forgiven us. God knows our desires. God will purify our love. God will give us the vision He has for us—not worrying about what we cannot help, but doing the things we can help and the things we should do that God wants to be done. We should know the difference, for God will know the difference, and do not doubt it.

Joke: *Once I knew a fellow who built himself a car. Someone asked him where he got the car, and he said he got the biggest piece at the city dump. But it would run. His wife said it would run too fast, and she asked him to slow down in fear that he would kill them all. He replied to his wife, "You are going as fast as I am." One day he was by himself and tried to make a curve too fast; consequently he ran over and down the hill. It was a rough and rocky ride down the hill. Since the driver was a very religious man, he was asked by someone if the Lord was with him. He said, "A' lordy, I don't know, but if He was He sure got a rough ride."*

Joke: *One time some folks were having a farm meeting, and they got an out-of-town speaker with impressive credentials. The speaker had all kinds of college degrees to his name. The old boy that was introducing the speaker would have been all right and done a good job if he had not called the letters of the degrees. When he finished the letters he said, "I don't know what they mean, but if it was left with us farmers I would say he is a registered critter."*

What is the meaning of life? I cannot answer that—for that has been the goal of human thought throughout all the ages. But I know the meaning of one life, Jesus, and it was love—a love that would comfort, support, forgive and save. It was not a love of earth but a love of heaven. It was not a love of man but a love of God. It was not a love that came and went. It was not a love that breaks hearts and breaks homes. It was not a love to be lost but a love to be saved. It was not a love to tear down but a love to build. It was not a love to get but a love to give. It was a love to go about doing good works. That was what Jesus did: He went about doing good deeds for others.

The deeply religious people of His day and time—the ones that held the religion in their hands—slurred Jesus and called Him the friend of sinners. They said this because Jesus associated with people considered by some as no account, or they had no use for them.

But the self-righteous religious people had to admit they never heard a preacher like Him, for He spoke with such power yet with such love and understanding. Jesus could look at men and see what was in them. He saw their conflicts, tensions and weaknesses, but Jesus did not pounce upon them because of their sins. With love and understanding the Savior would show them a new and better way of life. In Christ was God, reconciling the world unto Himself. But the world, allied against Christ and His disciples, attempted to keep the kingdom of God and His will from being done here on earth. This is an ancient curse and a present shame.

"The Lord is not slack concerning his promise, as some men count slackness; but is longsuffering to usward, not willing that any should perish, but that all should come to repentance" (John 3:9).

It is still God's will that all mankind should repent and be saved—for this is the Christian faith of every child of God in all the world—but it is not the will of all men. What can mean more to mankind than to realize that God came down to man's world, in the form of Jesus, to be man's Savior and to walk daily with man. God later sent the Holy Spirit as a comforter.

"And I, if I be lifted up from the earth, will draw all men unto me" (John 12:32). **But the Comforter, which is the Holy Ghost, whom the Father will send in my name, he shall teach you all things, and bring all things to your remembrance, whatsoever I have said unto you. Peace I leave with you, my peace I give unto you: not as the world giveth, give I unto you. Let not your heart be troubled, neither let it be afraid"** (John 14:15).

Prayer: *May all the people of every nation hunger and thirst after righteousness until they have a deep desire to do Thy will. For then and only then will they become interested in humanity and the problems of the human race. Save the lost and strengthen the saved. In Christ we do now pray. Amen.*

Notes

Chapter 1: Grace and Forgiveness
1. See 2 Corinthians 12:9.

Chapter 2: Better to Wear Out Than Rust Out
1. See John 14:15.
2. See John 15:14.
3. See Matthew 7:7.
4. See Matthew 9:13.
5. See Matthew 5:8.

Chapter 3: A Child and Childish Behavior
1. See Luke 18:8.
2. See John 14:15.
3. See John 15:14.
4. See Matthew 4:19.
5. See Matthew 5:8.

Chapter 4: Big Things and Little Things
1. See John 15:13.
2. See Proverbs 22:6.
3. See Ecclesiastes 12:1.
4. See Exodus 20:12.

Chapter 5: The World Offers Many Different Choices
1. See Proverbs 4:23.

Chapter 6: Prayer and Growth
1. See 1 Corinthians 9:25.
2. See Psalm 9:17.
3. See John 16:13.
4. See Proverbs 14:12.

Chapter 7: The Kingdom of Christ
1. See John 3:16.

Chapter 8: The Nature and Nurture of Children
1. See John 3:3.

Chapter 9: Second Birth: Spiritual Birth
1. See John 3:16.
2. See Matthew 6:10.
3. See Matthew 5:8.
4. See Psalm 37:25.

Chapter 10: A Few of the Many Dangers
1. See 1 Peter 2:22.
2. See 1 Corinthians 6:19.

Chapter 11: If We Do or If We Fail to Do
1. See Matthew 5:15.

Chapter 12: Leaving Spirit, Dangerous Road
1. See Luke 15:18-19.
2. See Luke 12:40.
3. See John 12:32.
4. See Luke 11:1-2.

Chapter 13: Come, Follow, Tarry and Go

1. See Matthew 11:28.
2. See Luke 24:49.
3. See Matthew 28:20.
4. See Matthew 16:24.
5. See Matthew 4:19.
6. See John 14:15.
7. See John 15:12.
8. See John 15:14.
9. See Matthew 9:13.
10. See John 11:25-26.
11. See Philippians 1:21.
12. See Genesis 1:28-29.
13. See Matthew 10:7-8.

Chapter 14: Faith: The Power of Salvation
1. See John 3:16.
2. See Matthew 11:19.
3. See Matthew 24:30-31.
4. See Matthew 3:16-17.

Chapter 15: Read Bible, Pray, Minister to Others
1. See John 3:16.
2. See Matthew 5:17.
3. See Luke 19:10.
4. See Mark 2:17.
5. See John 10:10.
6. See John 11:25-26.
7. See John 8:12.
8. See Romans 10: 13-15.
9. See Matthew 4:19.
10. See John 13:34.

Chapter 16: Doing All Things Well
1. See Matthew 25:21.
2. See Proverbs 4:23.

Chapter 17: Infinity of Influence: Good or Bad
1. See Isaiah 35:8.

Chapter 18: Jesus: a Friend to Mankind
1. See Matthew 5:9.
2. See Romans 6:22-23.
3. See Revelation 22:16-17.
4. See Luke 23-34.

Chapter 19: God's Still, Small Voice
1. See John 12:23.
2. See John 12:32.
3. See Revelation 2:10.
4. See Luke 13:43.
5. See Matthew 6:10.
6. See John 8:44.

Chapter 20: Attaining Success in Life
1. See John 8:42-43.
2. See John 8:46-47.

Chapter 21: Deathbed Repentance
1. See Ecclesiastes 12:1.
2. See Matthew 10:32.
3. See Revelation 2:10.
4. See Matthew 5:1-9.
5. See Matthew 9:13.
6. See Luke 19:10.

Chapter 22: Life: One Long School Day
1. See Mark 10:21.
2. See Luke 13:34.
3. See Matthew 23:12.
4. See Proverbs 14:34.
5. See John 16:13.

Chapter 23: A Good Harvest and a Good Life
1. Proverbs 14:34.
2. See John 4:14.
3. See John 6:37.
4. See Revelation 3:20.
5. See Luke 11:9.
6. See Luke 9:23.

Chapter 24: Sojourners in This Life
1. See Revelation 20:12.
2. See Matthew 5:8-9.

Chapter 25: Life Out of Death
1. See Luke 21:24.
2. See Luke 14:11.

Chapter 26: Jesus: An Understanding Savior
1. See Matthew 15:16.

Chapter 27: Position, Power, Wealth and Great Fortune
1. See Matthew 5:19.
2. See Matthew 8:10-12.
3. See Romans 6:23.
4. See Joshua 24:15.
5. See Matthew 5–7.
6. See Matthew 5:1-9.

Chapter 28: The Abundant Life
1. See Luke 17:21.
2. See Isaiah 55:10-11.
3. See John 10:1-11.
4. See Job 19:1-29.
5. See Matthew 18:11.
6. See Matthew 3:15.
7. See Matthew 9:12-13.

8. See Luke 19:10.
9. See John 14:6.
10. See John 11:25-26.
11. See Mark 16:15-16.
12. See Revelation 7:17.
13. See Revelation 21:4.

Chapter 29: Jesus: The Greatest Physician

1. See John 14:15.
2. See John 15:14.
3. See Philippians 4:13.
4. See Matthew 16:24.

Chapter 30: God: Man's Best Friend

1. See Matthew 5:9.
2. See 2 Peter 3:9.
3. See Genesis 1:31.

Chapter 31: The Meaning of Jesus' Life

1. See Galatians 6:9.
2. See 1 Thessalonians 5:9-10.W
3. See Ecclesiastes 12:13-14.
4. See Joshua 24:15.
5. See John 3:9.
6. See John 12:32.
7. See John 14:15.

Printed in the United States
102987LV00003B/166-999/A